Sonoma & Mendocino

SONOMA & MENDOCINO

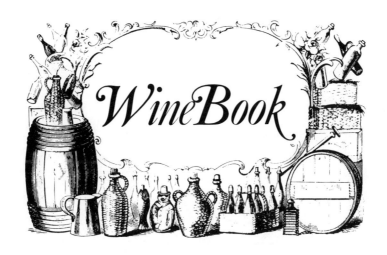

WineBook

Written by

Patricia Latimer

Illustrations by

Sebastian Titus

A Vintage Image Book

Table of Contents

Historical Perspective

To the north of San Francisco is a land of golden hills, rushing streams and grassy valleys. As a vast and relatively undeveloped frontier, the 5,085 square mile Sonoma-Mendocino region often seems forgotten by the people of California and the historians who write about it. Throughout its development, the area has been deeply bound to the history of California and an unusual mixture of Indians, homesteaders, gold diggers, freebooters, soldiers, conquistadors and oenophiles. It was here California was born.

In 1542, Juan Rodriquez, a celebrated Portuguese adventurer, departed Navidad, a small port south of Puerta Vallerta in Mexico, on an exploratory voyage along the coast of California. Somehow never seeing the Golden Gate, he found Point Concepcion, Point Reyes and finally Cape Mendocino further up the California coast. He christened his last stop in honor of the Mexican-based patron, Viceroy Antonio de Mendoza. Thus today this area bears the familiar county and village name, Mendocino.

More than 200 years later in 1775, navigator of the Spanish navy, Lt. Juan Francisco de la Bodega Y Quadra, anchored his ship, the Sonora, in a well-protected coastal bay which would later become Bodega Bay in Sonoma County.

Meanwhile in 1776, a group of Catholic missionaries from Mexico embarked on one of the first overland exploratory expeditions into the area north of San Francisco. There they found a series of Pomo, Miwok and Wappo Indian settlements which were scattered throughout the more fertile regions. Long before the missionaries arrived, the aboriginal Indians had made the Sonoma-Mendocino wilderness their home.

Around 1799, the Russians founded a fur trading colony in Sitka, Alaska. Difficulties arose by 1806 when the Czarist settlers were faced with acute shortages of basic supplies which were insufficient to maintain the colony. So bad were the conditions that Nicolai Rezanof, the imperial inspector of the colony, looked to California for new sources of food.

It was not until 1809, however, that a group of Russians led by Alexander Kushoff explored the areas now known as Sonoma and Mendocino counties. Establishing the first permanent settlement north of San Francisco in 1812, the Russians located themselves above a natural harbor 30 miles north of Bodega Bay and 13 miles northwest of the mouth of the Russian River. Once the site of a Pomo Indian village, the place was christened simply Ross, an archaic name for Russia. The Russians were the first to cultivate grape vines in the Sonoma region, using cuttings brought from the Black Sea area.

The Russians' attempt to establish a colony north of San Francisco threatened the Spanish authorities, who feared that the Russians wanted to gain control of all of California. As the southernmost settlement of the Czarist empire in North America, this appeared a true attempt to colonize what is now the western United States. The Russian occupation was a problem for Spain and Mexico until the colony was sold in 1841 to Captain John Sutter of Sacramento Valley fame.

California was a province of Spain until February 1821, when Mexico gained its independence from the motherland. Because of poor communications, nothing was really known of this situation in California. Although some government officials may have suspected it, word of the Independence move did not reach California Gov. Luis Arguello until almost a year later in January, 1822.

Whatever territorial intentions the Russians may have had for expansion, their plans were seriously challenged by the implacable wording of the Monroe Doctrine. In Dec. 23, 1823, President James Monroe asserted "that the American continents . . . are henceforth not to be considered as subjects for colonization by any European powers."

In that same year, the last of the Franciscan missions was built, Mission San Francisco de Solano. Originally there was no intention on the part of the Mexicans to found another mission, but several factors led to its establishment. Governor Arguello, the first Mexican governor born in California, was so disturbed by the Russian colonization efforts along the northern California coastline that he asked Father Jose' Altimira to hurry his plan to establish the new facility in Sonoma. Arguello felt that the mission would not only extend the church's religious influence, but act as a counter-force to possible Russian adventurism.

The Mission San Francisco de Solano was the last in a series of Franciscan enclaves which taught the "heathen" Indians western religion, education and agriculture. Located on the King's Highway, the "Camino Real," the missions were situated a day's journey apart by horse and wagon and extended from San Diego to Sonoma in northern California.

The original Mission San Francisco de Solano was a rough, temporary wooden structure which was gradu-ally replaced with a more permanent Spanish style building with adjacent wood and adobe structures as well as a granary.

In the decade following 1823, Mexico was faced with the problem of finding an effective permanent form of government for California. Territorial legislatures were set up, and Monterey was selected as the capital in Northern California. In that period, Gov. Jose' Figueroa, a gentleman prominent in Mexican politics, replaced Gov. Arguello. Also concerned about the ever increasing size and strength of the Russian settlement, the new governor decided to take action against it.

Gov. Figueroa investigated the background of one Mariano Guadalupe Vallejo as a possible appointee to take command of the Mission San Francisco de Solano. Something of a child prodigy, Vallejo displayed an interest in religion, politics, and world affairs at an early age. At 15, he began his military service as a cadet in the Presidial Company of Monterey, and thus was launched an illustrious military career. Rising rapidly through the ranks to corporal, sergeant and before long ensign, he helped quell a variety of Indian uprisings and also led a surveying party north of San Francisco through unexplored wilderness regions.In 1831, Vallejo was named commander of the San Francisco Presidio.

After Vallejo toured the Russian settlement at Ft. Ross in 1833, he realized the economic potential and political importance of occupying the land north of San Francisco. Enthusiastically, he reported to his superiors that the grassy, stream-fed Santa Rosa Valley and other neighboring areas were ideal for great ranchos

Ancient Zinfandel Vine

Mount St. Helena

and large herds of cattle. That the Russians sought only a base for fur trade and food sources seemed like a problem that could be resolved.

A year later, Gov. Figueroa, under the orders of the Mexican government, issued the Decree of Secularization which overthrew the authority of the Franciscan fathers and divided the mission property among the Indians, the church and the public. Gov. Figueroa named Vallejo as the commander of the Pueblo de Sonoma and civilian administrator of secularization for the Mission San Francisco de Solano in 1834.

Vallejo's colonization program was firmly established by 1835. The town of Sonoma was designed around a central plaza with a church and other residential dwellings and commercial buildings. Although the new leader encouraged settlers to come to Sonoma, the town's development was slow.

Vallejo became a general under a rather bizarre set of circumstances in 1836 when Mexican Nicolas Gutierrez was appointed governor and there developed a strong local sentiment against officials imported from Mexico. Shortly after the new governor took office, he threatened to dissolve the territorial legislature in Monterey. One of its leading members and opponents of such an idea was Alvarado Vallejo, the nephew of Mariano Vallejo, who with his cohort José' Castro, decided to prepare for their own rather personal revolution.

In great haste, Alvarado Vallejo headed to Sonoma, where he hoped to solicit the support of his uncle. Much to the young man's surprise, Mariano Vallejo was not in favor of revolution, but preferred preservation of peace on the northern frontier. Dismayed, but still determined, Alvarado left for Monterey. Half-way-there, he decided to go ahead with the revolution, proclaiming it in "Mariano Guadalupe Vallejo's name." With Castro's assistance, young Alvarado assembled an army of men, captured the town of Monterey and demanded Gov. Gutierrez's surrender. As head of the new government and president of the new legislature, Castro nominated the by-then Lt. Vallejo as the General of the free and sovereign state of California.

Vallejo's rather heavy-handed but nonetheless charming personality stimulated a mixed reaction of admiration and hatred among his associates. Prior to his visit to Ft. Ross, Vallejo had been openly accused of cruelty to the Indians. However, his policy changed when he realized that, if he befriended the Indians, they would not only act as a deterrent against outside aggression, but be less likely to harass the new settlers Vallejo was encouraging to homestead in the northern frontier.

An article written in the *New York Herald* explains the tenor of the Mexican government at that time.

"The stupidity of the people and the selfishness and tyranny of their military officers and government have reduced Mexico to the lowest grade of degradation and infamy. The sun never shone on a more beautiful country and God of Nature never dispensed his favors to a greater degree than he has on this now unfortunate country. Yet not withstanding these natural advantages, Mexico from certain causes, is now the meanest and lowest in the category of nations. Her people are ruled with a rod of iron and sunk in imbecility and infamy. Her military leaders are the most despotic

Cabernet Sauvignon Cluster

Sebastian Titus

and mercenary that ever exercised power; through effects of successive revolutions, all confidence of government is gone. She is without an army or navy and her coffers are empty. There is a never-ending struggle by a set of designing men to attain management of highest affairs and the only principle that guides them is self-aggrandizement."

When James K. Polk became president of the United States in 1845, he was determined to acquire California by purchase or seizure. At that time, war with Mexico was anticipated and considered by some a virtual certainty.

By 1846, American pioneer families had begun to cross the rugged Sierra Nevada in increasingly large numbers to settle much of California including many parts of Sonoma County. These early settlers were attracted by stories and promises of opportunity in the western lands. The pioneers were deeply disappointed when they realized they had been misled in their hopes. There was no prosperity; there was no free land. Instead the Americans found Gen. Vallejo, a ruthless Mexican officer ruling in a virtually despotic manner and using his vast military power to control the people.

The American settlers lived in an atmosphere which was exacerbated by the repeated onerous edicts of the Mexican government. Americans were prohibited from owning land. Another time, all "foreigners", namely Americans, were ordered expelled from the country and asked to leave their weapons behind. As the situation worsened, the normally peaceful immigrants finally rallied to defend their lands and their lives. The incidents thus provoked were the first of a series of confrontations which led to the Bear Flag Revolt on June 14, 1846, in which mostly American citizens rebelled against Mexican authority and tried to establish an independent republic.

Less than a year earlier, United States surveyor and explorer Captain J. C. Fremont and a group of 60-odd Indian guides, surveryors, and mountain men including Kit Carson, were on an exploratory mission to discover a short, practical route across the mountains to the Pacific. When they arrived in Monterey, the capital of the northern frontier, Fremont and his men received a warm reception from Gen. Castro. Fremont even obtained permission from Castro to conduct further expeditions in northern California. However, Fremont failed to obey Castro's request to by-pass the more populated and settled areas. Whatever Fremont's motives may have been remain a source of historical controversy and have not been firmly clarified. What is known is that barely a week passed after the Monterey visit before Fremont received orders from Castro to leave California at once. Fremont refused to comply.

Almost simultaneously, word reached Fremont from Washington, D.C., to situate himself at some point convenient to land and naval forces due to arrive in and around San Francisco. War with Mexico seemed inevitable. Fremont returned to the Sacramento Valley, not far from Sonoma or San Francisco.

On June 14, 1846, in the early morning, a group of anti-Mexican settlers at the advice of Fremont, stole the horses of Francisco Circe, which he was collecting for the forces which Gen. Castro was establishing in case of fighting in the northern frontier. Soon after, the

Americans rode together to the town of Sonoma where they surrounded the palatial residence of Gen. Vallejo and seized him and members of his family.

The rebels organized and elected one William B. Ide as their leader and established their own independent republic, modeling their new government after Texas. In celebration, the victors raised their homemade flag, a piece of unbleached muslin decorated with a brown bear, and flew it for nearly a month in Sonoma.

News of the Bear Flag Revolt travelled to John Fremont at Sutter's fort. Apparently recognizing an opportunity to further his ever present political ambitions and and probably feeling somewhat obligated to look out for the welfare of the rebels at Sonoma, who he believed were in imminent danger of Mexican reprisal, Fremont moved his whole camp to Sonoma. The band of mountain men arrived in Sonoma on June 25. From that day on, with the implied consent of the Bear settlers, Fremont was in command.

On July 6, 1846, Commodore John D. Sloat of the U.S.S. Portsmouth arrived off the coast of Monterey with the news of the war between Mexico and the United States. Soon thereafter, the Stars and Stripes was raised on the American Customs House in Monterey and three days later Old Glory was flying a-top the mast in the Sonoma plaza.

The development of the wine and grape industry in Sonoma-Mendocino has played an important part in the California wine story. From 1850 to 1900, this region was the center of history and culture. It was settled by an influential and imaginative group of wine pioneers such as Gen. Mariano G. Vallejo, Col. Agoston Harasz-thy, Samuel Orr, Louis Finne and other individuals who not only participated in the growth of Sonoma-Mendocino, but who are responsible for the achievements of this great North Coast wine district.

The first agriculturists in Sonoma County were the Russians, who in 1812 came to California and established a permanent colony north of Bodega Bay where they planted vegetables, orchards and vineyards. The Russians' grape growing and winemaking activities indicated the potential of developing the grape culture in the northern part of the state.

In 1824, when Father Altimira came north to found the Mission San Francisco de Solano, he planted the very popular Mission grapes, the original grapes planted by the Franciscan fathers. They were used for making a rather harsh-tasting wine. Records found at the mission reveal that the first vineyards tended by the priests yielded enough grapes to produce 1000 gallons of wine.

After the Decree of Secularization was passed in 1834, the Mexican government gained control over the California missions. The vineyards which Father Altimira had planted were taken over by Gen. Vallejo, who as the commander of the Pueblo de Sonoma expressed more than a passing interest in wine. As a measure to improve the quality of the wine which he wanted to make, Gen. Vallejo replanted the old vineyards with newer Mission grapes. The result of his early winemaking efforts was a moderately pleasing red wine.

Gen Vallejo's dedication to growing grapes and making wine so inspired friends, relatives and neighbors many of them joined him and settled in Sonoma

Russian River Valley

Riesling Grape Cluster

where they experimented with establishing the fruit culture. In 1839, the first woman to own and plant a vineyard in the Santa Rosa Valley was Senora de Carillo. In 1847, a gentleman by the name of Nicholas Carriger shipped new grape varieties from the East Coast called Muscats, Isabellas and Catawbas. His neighbor William Hill imported grape varieties such as Rose' of Peru, Italia, Black Hamburg and Golden Chasselas.

Although originally the settlement of Northern California was slow in developing, the unexpected discovery of gold in 1848 at James W. Marshall's mill in the foothills of the Sierra Nevada changed the complexion of California forever. Suddenly speculators came from around the world to seek great fortune. Their journeys took them inland to new and unexplored areas of the northern frontier. A short two years later, there were French, Italian, German, Spanish, Scottish and English settlers, all in search of gold. When the gold quest proved unrewarding, the immigrants turned to agriculture and viticulture. It wasn't until the late 1850's that the colonists became aware of the choice Sonoma-Mendocino land and the possibility of its development.

One of the most colorful personalities to settle in the Sonoma area was the dashing Col. Agoston Haraszthy de Moskea. Like Gen. Vallejo, Col. Haraszthy contributed to the development and knowledge of the wine industry in California. By importing grapes from Europe and making very high quality wines, he was able to convince members of the state legislature that California was capable of producing some of the best grapes in the world. The results of his experimental work in the vineyard and in the cellar in Sonoma not only proved his point, but, in the end, established the basis for a full-fledged grape and wine industry.

Col. Haraszthy was born on August 30, 1812 in Futtak, Hungary, to an aristocratic family. As a youngster, Agoston grew up in a time of political change when the Hungarian citizen was questioning the authority of the government particularly in respect to the rights of the individual. Experiencing a very conventional upbringing, the boy attended fine schools where the scholastic emphasis was on the law. By virtue of his station in life, he enlisted in the service of the royal guard, acting as executive secretary to the viceroy and living a country-gentlemanly way of life as a squire and grower.

In spite of these obvious advantages in life, Col. Haraszthy was a torn man. So sympathetic was he with the grievances of the commoners that he took up their cause and became a leader in the Hungarian nationalist movement. As the commoners' spokesman, he advocated liberty, justice and equality. Before long, his political activities provoked a reaction from the established powers and he had to flee his country for the States.

As one of the more talented individuals to come to America, Col. Haraszthy approached his new adventure with his characteristic enthusiasm. Barely settled, he wrote and published an informative book about America in Hungarian for the friends he had left behind. An instinctive entrepreneur, he carved a small empire out of the Wisconsin wilderness and founded Sauk City. There he built bridges, constructed roads, started schools, organized churches, entered politics

Sonoma Valley

and experimented in agriculture.

Unfortunately, Col. Haraszthy developed an asthmatic condition and in 1849 he left the cold winter-hot summer climate of Wisconsin for the sunnier and warmer climate of San Diego, California. Settling in the Mission Valley, Col. Haraszthy planted some of the first imported vines in the area. Involved in first local, then state politics, he served as sheriff, city marshal and state assemblyman.

In the late 1850's Col. Haraszthy moved north to San Francisco. As a wine grower in Crystal Springs near San Mateo, he imported and planted European varieties, but unfortunately he did not have much success. Heading farther north, he purchased an estate bordering on the Mission Dolores near San Francisco. Again, he had difficulties. The moist sea air and the cool summer fogs prevented his grapes from ripening properly, and he was forced to look for a more favorable location.

When Col. Haraszthy finally found a site in Sonoma County, he was convinced that the warm, sunny, dry climate was excellent for growing grapes. Selecting prime land, the suave promoter found a parcel of over 500 acres which was situated on the gently sloping hills of the Mayacamas Mountains. Very appropriately, he called his estate Buena Vista which means Beautiful View in Spanish. Surrounding the elegant villa he constructed were the vineyards, which were eventually made up of 85,000 vines of foreign and domestic varieties. At the time of Col. Haraszthy's relocation, Sonoma was fast becoming a major viticultural center.

Col. Haraszthy's contribution to the California wine industry lies in the depth and scope of his research, which was based on hitherto unpublished information. It was simplified and made available to the California grape grower. Firm in his convictions, Haraszthy believed in the pre-eminence of wine made from imported varieties. His reasoning was based on the results of experiments which showed that California had the finest climate, the best soil and the greatest growing season of any area in the world. In order that other wine growers could benefit from his knowledge, Col. Haraszthy published a comprehensive *Report on Grapes and Wine in California*. Later on he founded the Horticultural Society of Sonoma and wrote a book, *The Honored Guide of Grape Culture*.

Recognition of Haraszthy's work in the wine industry was brought to public attention when, in 1861, Gov. John G. Downey asked him to go to Europe. There, on behalf of the state of California, which was now interested in promoting the growth of the grape industry, the wine adventurer was to find sample cuttings of select varieties which could be grown at home. Delighted with his assignment, Col. Haraszthy left in June of that year. Staying for close to five months, he visited France, Italy, Germany, Spain and Russia. He returned with 200,000 plants of nearly 500 varieties. Due to the unfavorable political climate of the moment, namely Haraszthy's alleged support for Southern forces during the Civil War, the state legislature would not pay Col. Haraszthy for his trip. Thus he was forced to raise revenue and sell his plants to growers across the state.

As friendly neighbors, Gen. Vallejo and Col. Haraszthy enjoyed competing against each other in state and local fairs to see who could produce the most outstanding wines. From the beginning Vallejo's wines received the highest praise, but, as Col. Haraszthy became more skilled as a winemaker, he came up with some superior vintages. During one of the very early harvests at Buena Vista, Col. Haraszthy and his three sons Arpad (who studied wine and champagne making in France and later formed his own company); Attila and Gaza made 1000 gallons of wine. Pleased with their results, they sold it commercially for $2 a gallon.

It should be noted that Col. Haraszthy was by no means the first person to import foreign varieties to the United States. Europeans who had originally settled here had done so earlier and made fine wine besides. What Col. Haraszty did do was to make particular varieties more well-known.

At the end of that year, Sonoma County was the state's second largest wine district with 1,100,000 vines under cultivation. Los Angeles was first with 1,200,000 vines planted. The area known as the Sonoma Valley continued to develop as a center for the production of high quality, dry table wines. This growing interest in wine in Sonoma County attracted the interest and investment of winemakers from the major wine growing countries of the world.

Among the more famous wine growers who settled in the area were Emil Dresel and Jacob Gundlach, founders of the Gundlach Bundschu Wine Co. Dresel, who grew up in the town of Gisenheim on the Rhine, came from a German wine family. Gundlach, a native of Bavaria, had a father who was a hotel owner and wine grower. Together as partners they bought magnificent vineyards in the foothills of the Huichica Mountains near the town of Sonoma. The vineyard was called the Rhinefarm and provided grapes for the wine which was made at the winery for their San Francisco-based retail company, the Gundlach Bundschu Wine Co.

Another very important wine firm Kohler & Frohling established vineyards in Sonoma County in 1875. As early as 1854, Charles Kohler and John Frohling had founded their company in Los Angeles where they grew grapes and made wine. Also in that same year, they opened a small retail shop on Merchant St. in San Francisco. By 1860, the partners did so well that they started an agency in New York which distributed their California wines. By 1875 the firm purchased 800 acres of rolling countryside in Glen Ellen in the Sonoma Valley. The partners produced some of their finest dry table wines from their Tokay Vineyard made up of Mission, Muscat, Rose' of Peru, Golden Chasselas and Riesling. To store their wine, they constructed a stone winery, a distillery and sherry cellars. In 1910, this prime Glen Ellen property was sold to the then world-famous author, Jack London.

An intriguing name in California viticulture is Kanaye Nagasawa, the owner of the highly respected Fountain Grove Vineyard. Born of Japanese nobility, he reached his position as sole proprietor of the American firm by following the teachings of one Thomas Harris. A mystical prophet whom Nagasawa met in England, Harris led his students to live in religious colonies first in New York and later California.

In 1875, Harris purchased 1400 acres of land in the Santa Rosa Valley to be used as a dairy farm and vine-

Chardonnay grape cluster

yard. Planting fine strains of Zinfandel, Pinot Noir and Cabernet Sauvignon, he produced highly prized vines which were sold in the United States, Great Britain and Japan. Nagasawa became the owner in 1920 after Harris was forced to leave the area due to a scandal in the Santa Rosa religious colony. To this day, older vintages of Fountain Grove Vineyard wines are among some of the finest red wines Sonoma County has ever produced.

Extensive planting was the order of the day during the 1870's. By 1875, Sonoma County ranked as the number one producer in California with a production of 3,397,612 gallons. Los Angeles County which until then had always ranked number one, took second place with 3,238,900 gallons. As a result of this production glut, a year later wine was selling for the rock-bottom price of 10¢ a gallon.

By the early 1880's the economy had improved and Sonoma County was once again on the road to recovery. For most of the Sonoma vintners, these early years showed marked success. However, in the 1880's the ravages of pylloxera, an insect which destroys the roots of the grapevine, were being disastrously felt throughout the county (and the state). As early as 1873, pylloxera was found on Sonoma grapevines.

In the late 1870's Julius Dresel of the Gundlach-Bundschu Wine Co., did extensive experimental work in his vineyard at the Rhinefarm, grafting disease-prone vines onto pylloxera resistant rootstock. His work was instrumental in saving vineyards in that county and elsewhere.

In 1909, Carl Dresel, grandnephew of Julius Dresel, wrote George C. Husman, one of the gentlemen Leon D. Adams credits with arresting the pylloxera plague in California. This excerpt describes Julius Dresel's work with pylloxera.

"At this time (1875) the pylloxera valatrix had already begun to devastate the vineyards in the Sonoma Valley. Mr. Dresel with his characteristic energy worked day and night studying ways and means to combat the ravages of the pest. He soon came to the conclusion that ordinary methods of isolation, destruction of infested spots and chemical poisons were impracticable. He was of the belief that the only sure remedy consisted in finding a root that would not succumb to the attack of the louse (vine-pest). He was the first man in California to import wild roots from the Mississippi and Mission River bottom, plant them in his vineyards, and to test them thoroughly he planted them with the lice obtained from his diseased vines.

"The roots continued to thrive and verified his belief (that it was necessary to find a pylloxera-resistant rootstock). In the next few years, the entire vineyard died from the effect of the louse. As each block of vines disappeared, it was replanted with resistant roots and later grafted. The experiment was eminently successful. The first crop from vines grafted on resistant roots was pressed in 1878 and the same vines are bearing today, a period of 30 years."

From 1881 to 1895 owners of flourishing Sonoma County vineyards were selling their wine grapes and bulk wines for very low prices. Not only was the wine industry in a very precarious economic state, but the United States was in the middle of a depression. As a means of saving themselves from further ruin, several

Riesling grape cluster botrytis cinerea

major wine firms joined together to form the California Wine Association. Composed primarily of wine merchants, the organization set out to improve the general standard of wine and stabilize grape prices. The California Wine Association achieved its goals by enforcing established grower-winery contracts for grapes at fixed prices. Four of the original seven wineries in the association were located in Sonoma: Kohler & Frohling, who owned vineyards in Glen Ellen; B. Dreyfus & Co., who owned the Goldstein Vineyards in the Sonoma Valley and Arpad Haraszthy & Co.

Not too much later a rival syndicate, the California Winemakers' Corporation was formed. It was headed by John H. Wheeler, with the support of two other Italian Swiss Agricultural Colony supporters, Andrea Sbarboro and Pietro Rossi. Composed primarily of wine growers, the organization tried to stimulate the economy by encouraging grape growers to sell their grapes (or bulk wine) not just to one firm like the California Wine Association, but to numerous wine firms.

As Sonoma County developed into a viticultural center, it was settled by groups of people of various nationalities and cultures. With them, these immigrants brought the wisdom, love and laughter, as well as the cherished customs of their European homelands. One of the largest and most influential groups were the Italians. Between 1890 and 1919 there was a large settlement of Italians who lived between Healdsburg and Cloverdale and devoted most of their energies to winemaking. Traditionally, these growers and vintners would sell their wine to San Francisco wine firms or the aforementioned co-operatives or syndicates. Undaunt-

ed by the challenge of a new and sometimes strange land, these men worked hard creating their own American wine story. Some of the individuals who should be remembered are Giuseppe Mazzoni, Edward Seghesio, Andrew Sodini, John Foppiano, Samuele Sebastiani and others.

Prior to 1900, another group of immigrants established the French Colony in the rolling hills between Cloverdale and Asti. One Fred Vadon, now 80, and one of the last surviving members of the French Colony recalls the names of his childhood friends, all founders of their own wineries. They include his father Felician Vadon, Jules Leroux, Paul Leroux, Armand de Hay, Theodor de Hay, Louis Bee, Emil Bee, Gustave Provost and Ulysseus Zurcher.

In a very short time, these dedicated newcomers helped to lay the cornerstone of the Sonoma wine industry. Sonoma's chief claim to fame was as a producer of bulk wines (these are wines which are held in storage tanks prior to bottling or sale to another winery under another's label), however, some of the wineries bottled under their own label or private labels (wines to be sold by other wineries, wine shops or restaurants).

At the turn of the century winemaking became a fully recognized industry in Sonoma County. Just as the wine business began to expand, growers and vintners were threatened by temperance which cast dark shadows on their ambitions. From 1920, the start of Prohibition, growers were able to derive a healthy income from the sale of grapes for juice in eastern markets. This prosperity, however, was short-lived, and one by one wineries began to close down while only a few remained opened for medicinal and sacramental production.

Following Repeal of Prohibition in 1933, Sonoma County and other state districts experienced record grape harvests. Large firms prospered, bottling and selling wine nationally. Smaller family firms suffered when they were unable to crack the national market. The period following the Dry years was one of overproduction and the number of wineries in Sonoma County began to wane. By 1950, the list of producing wineries was at an all-time low.

The mid-sixties caught the American wine industry by surprise when consumption of dry table wines more than doubled in volume. Millions of Americans began to use dry table wines with meals, where before emphasis had been on sweet dessert consumption. By the early seventies, the average American was consuming approximately a gallon and a half per person, an unheard of amount for this country.

This increased demand set off unprecedented interest in vineyard and winery development in Sonoma County and around the state. Moneyed-interests, large national and international corporations, whiskey and importing conglomerates, wealthy investors in need of tax shelters poured billions of dollars in venture capital into old family firms, neglected wineries and new ventures.

By the mid-seventies the zest for planting resulted in drastically recessed grape prices. Nevertheless, dry table wine consumption proceeded to increase at a steady six percent annually. The advent of the eighties found the wineries well-prepared, having planted even more acreage and often quadrupling production, for a wine phenomenon this century has yet to witness.

The story of wine in Mendocino County, the Redwood Empire, dates from 1840. Talk of gold in the northern Ukiah valley attracted pioneers who when no gold was to be found settled the interior valleys, growing fruits, like grapes, raising grains, like hops as well as harvesting lumber. Although the climate was ideal for fruits and vegetables, the farmers were soon frustrated when their horse-drawn carts, their sole means of transportation to points south, could not get produce to markets fast enough. By the late 1850s the northern Ukiah Valley had become a profitable center of commercial grape growing.

Samuel Orr, a native of Kentucky, was believed to be one of the first to bring imported grape cuttings to Mendocino County in 1857, planting them in Reeves Canyon to the north of Ukiah. Shortly thereafter, Anson Jebidiah Seward, a gold seeker, bought cuttings from Orr and established vineyards in the Redwood Valley at the present site of Fetzer Vineyards. Then, in 1858, neighbor Berry Wright attempted but failed to produce vines in the same valley not far from Seward.

From 1859, the year Ukiah was made the county seat, it became an important center of commerce in the north. In the next twenty years, Mendocino County began to develop bulk wine concerns. In 1879, Prussian Louis Finne established the first Mendocino County winery on Uva Road in Calpella and made wine from Thompson Seedless grapes. By 1880 Mendocino

County records reported a total of 330 acres planted to vine. Pioneers like Finne, who gradually increased the size of his winery and markets, watched the industry grow as rail service was established between San Francisco and Ukiah and the Redwood Highway was completed. Soon wine was being shipped to markets as far away as New York and Washington, D.C.

In 1906, George Massoletti built the second winery in Calpella and planted and made Zinfandel. Immigrants like the Finns and the Scots followed, forming communal colonies and planting vineyards. Grape growing continued to boom through the Prohibition years and after, with new wineries springing up throughout the district.

Mendocino County, like northern Sonoma County, established a reputation based on its production of bulk table wines. The late sixties-early seventies changed this, when new premium varietal cuttings were introduced by firms such as Parducci Wine Cellars and Fetzer Vineyards. These plantings inspired development of new regions, the Anderson Valley not far from the Pacific Coast. Pioneer families like the Edmeades and Husches put fine regional estate wines on the map from coastal Mendocino County. The eighties marked still more growth and change as millions of dollars were invested in small concerns, often family owned and operated in areas like Hopland, McDowell Valley and Potter Valley. Winery and vineyard development in the last decade have made this county one of the top premium growing districts in the state.

The Wineries

California

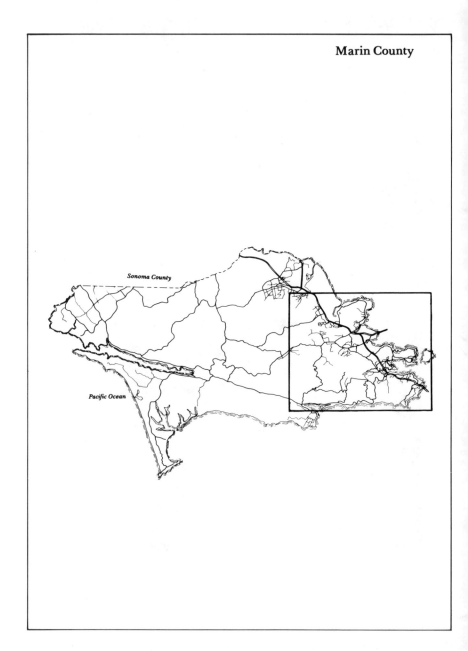

Marin County

Marin County Wineries

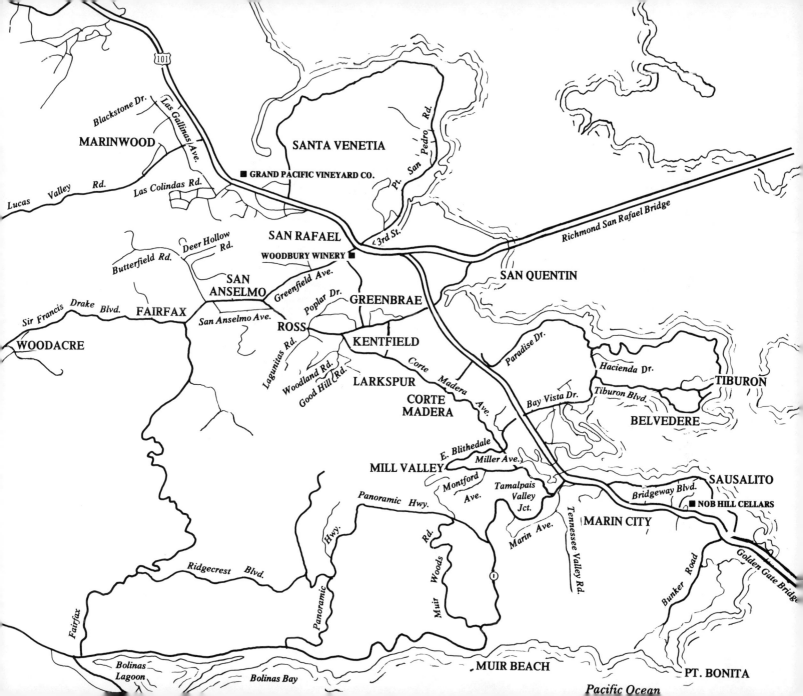

Marin Wineries

At the Lucas Valley exit off of the Redwood Highway in San Rafael is the Grand Pacific Vineyard Company. Dr. Richard Dye, a former professor in physiology and anatomy at the College of Marin, established his wine venture in 1975.

When Dye thought to start a winery, he was intrigued with Marin County's history as a producer of Cabernet Sauvignon. He began by buying grapes from the Dry Creek Valley. "I made but one wine, Merlot, from good and rare grapes," says Dye.

By the late seventies, Dye moved his operation to a winery in the Northgate Industrial Park, expanded his list, and produced close to 6,000 cases annually.

Today, the winery which takes its name from the old F. Korbel & Co. line of champagnes, produces medium-priced premium varietals, many of which are oak-aged. They include Chardonnay, Merlot, Cabernet Sauvignon and Pinot Noir, with some experimental work with a Gamay Saumon and an Eye of the Partridge Merlot. By the eighties, Dye hopes to develop a winery and vineyard site in the San Geronimo Valley not far from the Pacific Ocean.

Russell and Linda Woodbury are the owners and operators of the first, San Rafael-based, Marin County vintage portworks of the century.

Woodbury Winery, as the operation is so named, produced fewer than 600 cases in 1977; 1000 cases in 1978; and maximum production of 4,000 cases by 1985. Woodbury, a former marketing executive for the Cresta Blanca Winery, creates his ports (predicting at least seven vintage ports every decade due to the consistent California growing climates) from Petite Sirah, grown at hillside elevations. Future plans are to also experiment with Cabernet Sauvignon, Zinfandel and Pinot Noir compositions as substantial grapes from which to make full-bodied port wines.

Woodbury has expressed that many wineries throughout America are conditioned in their thinking to using grapes of lower quality, harvested at peaks of ripeness, for their ports. "They are often on the verge of turning to raisins," says Woodbury.

Woodbury Winery will emphasize classical ports, distinctive in taste, because of a character that resembled wine flavors vinified in a traditional port style.

NOB HILL CELLARS

Nob Hill Cellars, located at 200 Gate Five is Sausalito's newest winery. It is owned and operated by Gil Nickels of San Francisco.

The Marin County operation will begin by producing one wine, from the noble Chardonnay grape, grown in the southern Napa Valley. The grapes will be vinified in a traditional manner, regulated by temperature-controlled stainless steel fermentations, with emphasis on quality production and aged in small French oak cooperage.

"We're after the premium market," says Nickels, winemaker, advised by consulting enologist Chuck Ortmann. "We're more interested in complexity of the total wine than fruitiness in the bouquet or taste."

In 1979, the winery crushed 5,000 cases, with future expansion to level off at 20,000 cases annually. Available cork finished, 750 millilitre bottles of Chardonnay will retail for $8 to $12 a bottle. The wines will be sold throughout California and from the tasting room in Sausalito by prior appointment.

California

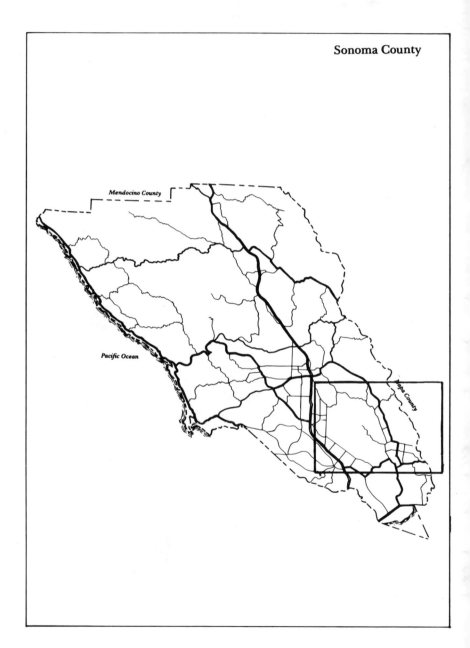

Sonoma County

Southern

Sonoma

Wineries

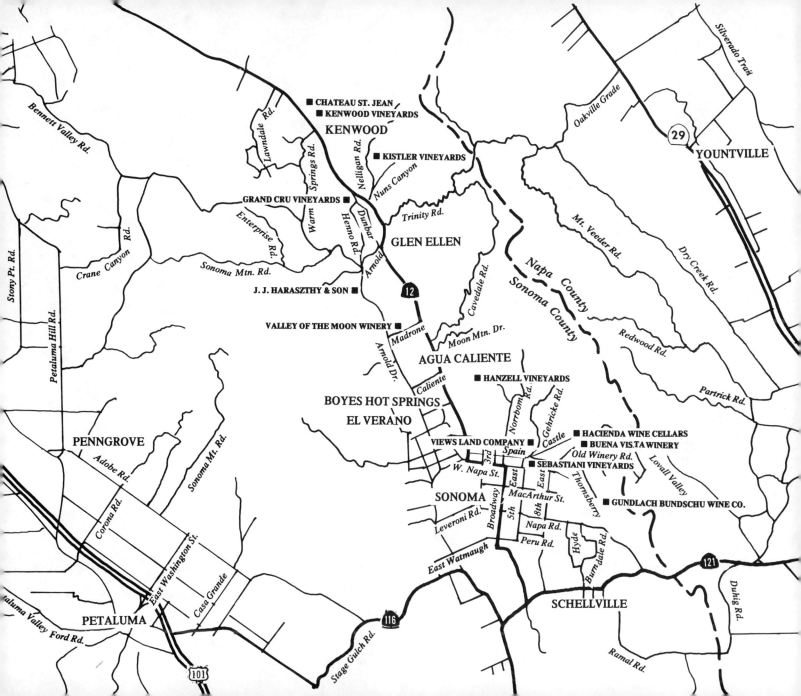

Gundlach Bundschu Wine Co.

The Gundlach Bundschu Wine Co., located along the foothills of the Huichica Mountains in the Sonoma Valley, is one of California's most venerable names in wine.

The vineyards date from 1855, when the German born team of Jacob Gundlach and his son-in-law, Emil Dresel, planted varietal grapes at their 400 acre Rhine Farm in Sonoma, California. The wine estate featured German, French and American varieties consisting of Riesling, Traminer, Gutedel, Kleinberger, Semillon, Zinfandel, Cabernet Sauvignon, Pinot Noir and Merlot.

By 1858, Gundlach and Dresel had formed the firm of J. Gundlach & Co. Sonoma County wines were produced from estate grapes made into wine at the 150,000 gallon stone winery (a magnificent volume in those days) and marketed under the Bachus label.

Charles Bundschu and Harry Winkle joined Gundlach and Dresel in 1864 to form the Gundlach Bundschu Wine Co. For nearly 50 years, the business continued to expand and successful wholesale and retail markets were established in New York and San Francisco. The 1906 earthquake in San Francisco virtually destroyed the three story wine vault of rare and old vintages belonging to the firm.

In the aftermath of the devastation and fire, the owners attempted to rebuild the Gundlach Bundschu Wine Co. Due to the experimental works in 1875 of Julius Dresel, one of the founders, their vineyards were spared from being totally destroyed by phylloxera (a vine pest which eats away at the roots of the grape vine). Dresel had successfully grafted some of the first disease prone vines onto phylloxera resistant rootstock at the Rhine Farm.

The vineyards continued to produce fruit through Prohibition, even though the winery was closed down. For the next 50 years or so, under the direction of great grandson Towle Bundschu, grapes were cultivated and sold commercially at the Rhine Farm.

In 1964, great great grandson James Bundschu and brother-in-law John Merritt, Jr., decided to revive the family wine firm. Three hundred acres of vines were replanted in 1968 from grafts from the original varieties and some additional ones. Cabernet Sauvignon, Merlot, Zinfandel, Pinot Noir, Chardonnay, Johannisberg Riesling, Gewurztraminer, Sylvaner and White Riesling are the predominant grape types.

Both Bundschu and Merritt hail the Sonoma Valley as an important and proven appellation of origin, which they hope to see recognized on a national basis. They point out that the growing conditions are unique to Sonoma County because of the rich soils, the mean temperature of 56 degrees Fahrenheit and the San Pablo Bay influence. Merritt uses Pinot Noir as an example to illustrate the area's effect on growing grapes. "It takes from seven to eight years for vines (such as the Pinot Noir) to mature in these light soils and cool districts," explains Merritt, the winemaker. "We average two to two and a half tons per acre of fruits with high acids and good sugars."

"Our goal," explains Merritt, "is to make wines that go well with food as that is the natural place to use wine."

Hacienda Wine Cellars

Hacienda
Wine Cellars

1976
Sonoma Valley
Cabernet Sauvignon

Estate Grown, Produced, and Bottled by
Hacienda Wine Cellars, Sonoma, California
Alcohol 12.5% by Volume

Hacienda Wine Cellars is a small premium winery in the western foothills of the Mayacamas Mountains in Sonoma, California. It is located on the historic Buena Vista Vineyards started by Count Agoston Haraszthy in 1862, and is among the first imported varietal vineyards in California.

Frank Bartholomew, while President of United Press International, bought the neglected wine estate at auction in 1941. With Andre Tchelistcheff, a noted American wine consultant, Bartholomew re-established the firm's name in the commercial marketplace with his first release of wine in 1949. In 1968, Bartholomew sold the stone Buena Vista Winery, and eight acres of surrounding vineyards to Young's Market in Los Angeles. On the remaining 450 acres of land he founded Hacienda Wine Cellars in 1973. Six years later the winery was incorporated and A. Crawford Cooley, a San Francisco venture capitalist, became principal investor and president. Cooley runs the winery; Bartholomew runs the vineyards.

Since its inception Hacienda Wine Cellars has been explained as "an experiment in quality and nothing else." This theme has been carried forth in all phases of the vineyard and winery operation. Zinfandel, and several other varieties, are grown on 70 acres at the Cooley Oat Valley Farm in Cloverdale, the warmest part of the county. Chardonnay, Johannisberg Riesling and Cabernet Sauvignon come from the 60 acres of estate vines at the winery, the coolest part of the county.

U.C. Davis graduate and winemaker Steven Mac Rostie points out that these two districts provide him with what he considers "the best possible grapes to make the best possible premium wines."

The Hacienda Winery, which is designed in a Spanish style of architecture with stucco walls, tile roof and outdoor balconies, used to be a hospital. It has been completely reconstructed with redwood timbers from Ft. Mason in San Francisco Bay. Surrounding the winery are stately pine trees and a shaded picnic area overlooking a lake. Downstairs in the winery are private bins where customers can cellar purchased wines at a modest fee.

Since the ownership change, expansion production is approaching 20,000 cases annually. Facilities have been enlarged to house additional stainless steel jacketed fermenters, stainless storage and more French and American small oak cooperage.

Hacienda wines have won medals and awards in competitions throughout the world. From the onset, Mac Rostie established a recognizable style that reflects simplicity and an identifiable technique that gets results. All the white wines (the one exception being the Chardonnay) are cold-fermented and stored in stainless steel to preserve the vitality of the grape and freshness of the fruit. The Gewurztraminer and Johannisberg Riesling are good examples of this method. The Chardonnay is aged in French Limousin oak, and has more overall complexity.

Buena Vista Winery

In a natural wooded glen beside the Arroyo Seco Creek east of Sonoma stands an imposing grey and stone structure. Over the entrance is a red and gold coat of arms with a drawn sword above a king's crown. Below are two large redwood doors bolted closed with an iron latch. The historic doors open to tell the story of Buena Vista Vineyards and the House of Haraszthy.

Buena Vista Winery and Vineyards dates from 1857 when it was founded by the dashing Col. Agoston Haraszthy de Moskea. As the oldest winery in the Sonoma Valley, it has often been regarded as the home of California winemaking.

Throughout his life Haraszthy was passionately involved in the cause of liberty and justice, and it was his concern for conditions of the common Hungarian under an oppressive monarchy that caused his exile. Although a high ranking army officer, Haraszthy found it necessary to escape from his native land in 1840 and flee to the United States.

Soon after landing on the eastern seaboard, the ever restless Haraszthy headed westward. He experimented and planted vineyards along the way — in Sauk, Wisconsin, and later in San Diego, California. His engaging personality and ability to get things done impressed people everywhere. His name appears on buildings, towns, parks, schools, roads, bridges and churches across the country. It wasn't until Haraszthy settled in Sonoma, however, that he was truly successful as a grape grower and winemaker.

While Haraszthy lived near San Francisco, Gen. Mariano Vallejo invited the count to visit his country residence, Lachryma Montis (Tear of the Mountain), and taste what are thought to be some of the first wines from the district. Impressed with the quality of these dry table wines Haraszthy began purchasing hillside acreage in and around the Mayacamas Mountains. There he built a magnificent Pompeiian villa and planted rootstock which became the backbone of this famous Buena Vista Winery & Vineyards (which means beautiful view in Spanish).

Haraszthy established his winery as a private family enterprise, but later it was incorporated and renamed the Buena Vista Vinicultural Society. It gained a reputation as a leader in the wine industry from the onset. It was one of the first wineries to experiment with imported varietals and to use sophisticated equipment with its application to advanced technologies. The winery had some of the first automated crusher-stemmers, quality fermenters, redwood storage tanks and small European oak cooperage. Six caves were dug into the limestone hillsides and used as aging cellars for the wine. During these first few years of operation Haraszthy popularized the Zinfandel grape and dispelled the myth that the Mission grape was the only one from which to produce wine in California.

From 1861, when Haraszthy traveled abroad to visit the great chateaux of Europe and purchased

Old Champagne Cellars at Buena Vista

sample cuttings, his ideas and activities would have a major impact on the development of the California wine industry. Upon returning he brought 200,000 plantings of nearly five hundred varieties from major wine districts throughout France, Germany, Italy and Spain. These *vitis vinifera* varieties would later become the basis of the California wine industry.

As the Buena Vista Vinicultural Society grew it experienced continual internal strife and eventually ran into problems due to financial difficulties. In the middle 1800s Haraszthy resigned as head of the organization and left California for Nicaragua. Again using his imagination and abilities, he was able to secure a commission from the Nicaraguan government to plant sugar cane, build a distillery and manufacture rum. Quite unexpectedly it was later reported that Haraszthy while on one his missions died in a drowning. Gaza Haraszthy, one of his three sons, was left to manage the South American rum operation and Arpad and Attila Haraszthy, his other two sons, were left to run the North American wine operation.

In the following years, Buena Vista Winery & Vineyards earned a reputation for its Eclipse Champagne and dry table wines. By the late 1890s however, the phylloxera plague (a vine pest that destroys the roots of the grape vine) which swept Sonoma County had wiped out Haraszthy's vineyards. No sooner were

they replanted than they were hit by the 1906 earthquake. The heavy tremors toppled the limestone caves and took the wine inventory with it. From then on, the winery was officially closed for almost four decades.

In 1941, Frank Bartholomew, then President of United Press International, revived the Buena Vista Winery & Vineyards. He hired the talented enological expert, Andre Tchelistcheff, to advise him on winemaking procedures. By the early fifties, Buena Vista Green Hungarian, Zinfandel, and Gewurztraminer were on wine lists in major restaurants and hotels across the country.

Twenty-seven years later in 1968 Young's Market of Los Angeles, a wholesale wine and liquor firm, bought the original Buena Vista stone winery buildings and eight acres of surrounding Gewurztraminer and Johannisberg Riesling. Production stayed at 20,000 cases annually.

During the seventies, President Philip Gaspar, with the help of Chilean-born technical director Rene La Casia, established a masterplan which would increase production to 175,000 cases by the late eighties. An expensive modern complex was constructed and equipped at the new winery site on Ramal Road at the base of the Sonoma Valley. Plantings of 650 acres of premium varietals were developed and will be fully bearing in 1985.

Sebastiani Vineyards

Sebastiani Vineyards lie on the historic locus of the first vineyard cultivated north of San Francisco. The vines were planted in 1825 by Franciscan padres at the Mission San Francisco de Solano in Sonoma. Following the Act of Secularization, which ended the Church's reign over the mission system and replaced it with Mexican authority, the vineyard was acquired by General Mariano G. Vallejo.

Samuele Sebastiani had been born into a peasant family who toiled in the vineyards of Tuscany. Short of formal education (he never did learn to write English) and impatient with a sharecropper's existence, in 1892 he borrowed money for steerage to California. He worked in the vegetable gardens of San Francisco, then moved north to Sonoma. A diligent worker, fond of physical exertion, he bought a stout cart and a team of horses and began hauling cobblestones from the quarries in the Mayacamas Mountains east of town. Sonoma's City Hall, a regional landmark, was built by Italian immigrants, who Sebastiani sponsored, and largely with cobblestones Sebastiani quarried and hauled.

In 1904, he purchased an old horse-barn-turned winery at the northeast corner of town and the Franciscan Vallejo vineyard across the street. Visitors to the winery today are shown the hand crusher, hand basket press, and 501 gallon redwood tank Samuele and his uncle used to make the winery's first Zinfandel. When the wine was aged, Samuele sold it door to door from barrels on his horse-drawn wagon.

During the unwelcome intrusion of Prohibition he kept the winery alive by producing sacramental and medicinal wines. He also set up a fruit and vegetable cannery next door to keep his employees at work and protect his investment. At Repeal Samuele's youngest son, August, left college to run the family business. He learned to make the big, sharp on the tongue, full-bodied reds that are so characteristic of Italian wines. And, as was the custom then, the wines were sold to larger wine merchants like Lachman & Jacobi, who resold them under myriad labels, none of which directly mentioned the wines' true origin.

After Samuele's death in 1944, the complexion of the winery changed slowly at first. By the early fifties August had begun to produce wines for his own label. The story leading up to the move is best told by August himself.

"One day my wife, Sylvia, returned from an afternoon of bridge. She commented on the pale dry cocktail sherry her hostess had served and asked why we did not make such a wine. It was my wine, under someone else's label. It really bothered me that I couldn't even get credit from my own wife. That's when I knew it was time for a change."

August is proud that both his sons have joined him in running the winery. Sam's primary obligations are management, but he likes to get into the vineyards as often as his hectic schedule will allow. Don, the

Aging Cellars at Sebastiani Vineyards

youngest of August's three children, is learning the business by working as his father's assistant. The brother-in-law Dick Cuneo, is the winery's controller.

August has gained a notoriety for the custom-tailored blue and white striped, bib overalls he habitually wears. But it is no pose. The man is a farmer by love and a businessman by necessity.

Anyone taken into August's comfortable dress is liable to be taken for a fascinating—August is charming and witty—but financially unrewarding ride. For August Sebastiani couples a vast reservoir of knowledge and experience with a keen, native sense of timing. Before the rise of consumer sophistication in the early seventies, he had already begun vintage dating his top varietals. When the demand came, he had the wines. When prices got out of hand, he hit the market like a tidal wave in half gallons at markedly lower prices. In 1972, he started an American tradition, albeit borrowed from France, with his Nouveau Gamay Beaujolais, a fruity, tantalizing red meant to be drunk within several months of its production. People make special trips to Sonoma to obtain the Nouveau when it is released annually on November 15th.

From a position of producing less than 300,000 cases of wine a year in the early seventies, Sebastiani Vineyards now produces close to three million cases each vintage. And as long as the Sebastiani name has been known to wine lovers, the name Barbera has been an appendage to it. It is the wine that links the American Sebastianis with their European homeland. The Sebastiani Barberas, like many Italian wines (though not, curiously those made with Barbera), are designed to stand up to the most heavily spiced of foods. The label says "Bold and Robust," and so the wines are.

The Sebastianis offer a complete line of table wines, dessert, aperitif and sparkling wines. To name them all would be superfluous, but a few deserve special mention. One is their American Solera Cream Sherry, dubbed "Amore." The Sebastianis maintain an outdoor solera of 2400 50-gallon oak barrels to fractionally blend and age their sherries. The sun's heat bakes the wines slowly, carmelizing existing sugars, giving the Cream Sherry a deep, creamy, amber color, a thicker consistency and delightful nut-like flavors. In 1977 the winery released another fractionally blended wine that had almost been forgotten it had been in the winery so long. Labeled "Angelica Antigua," a mere 353 cases were bottled, individually numbered and sold at $30 a fifth. The wine reminds one of peach cobbler.

Another interesting wine is Pinot Noir Blanc, subtitled "Eye of the Swan" for its copper cast, like unto the eye color of the Black Australian Swan in August's aviary (he is an internationally known breeder of rare doves).

With the advent of the eighties, the winery continues to expand with no apparent end in sight. As it does, the Sebastianis continue to enlarge their wood and bottle aging facilities. While many whites and light-bodied reds are soon sold after bottling, the heavier reds continue to receive two to three years in redwood and oak and an additional year in bottle before release.

Hanzell Vineyards

1971

Hanzell
SONOMA VALLEY
PINOT NOIR

Grown and Bottled at the Winery by
HANZELL VINEYARDS, SONOMA, CALIFORNIA
BONDED WINERY #4470 · ⅘ QUART · ALCOHOL 13% BY VOLUME

A long road winds its way past oak, olive and oleander through trellised vineyards to a promontory overlooking the Sonoma Valley. There on a hilltop stands Hanzell Vineyards, a replica of Clos de Vougeot in Burgundy, built to miniature scale.

This multimillionaire's fancy was the inspiration of the late James Zellerbach, heir to the San Francisco paper fortune and one-time ambassador to Italy. His love for France and the fine wines of Burgundy's Cote d'Or—lovely Montrachets and Romanee Contis—developed while Zellerbach lived in Europe in the forties. By the late forties, when he returned to America, he had but one dream—to build a splendid California winery on 200 acres of rolling Sonoma countryside and make unsurpassable Burgundian style wines. For Californians, he wanted to produce Pinot Noir and Chardonnay in the tradition of the chateau concept."

Naming his winery "Hanzell," he cleverly combined Hannah Zellerbach's first name with James Zellerbach's last name. Beautifully terraced vineyards were planted under exacting conditions. The finest clones were selected and planted in redhill clay loams with southwestern exposure.

Nearly two decades after the founding, following Zellerbach's death, Mr. and Mrs. Douglas Day of Sacramento bought Hanzell. Since 1975, Countess Barbara de Brye, a Cambridge-educated Australian heiress, has owned the winery. With her husband Jacques, a Parisian banker, she spends her time between the United States and Europe.

Hanzell Vineyards has been unique since its inception because both the winery and vineyards are designed on a "small scale to ensure maximum quality." Within the last few years, de Brye has invested new capital in vineyard plantings bringing total acreage up to 32: 15 acres of Pinot Noir; 12 acres of Chardonnay; and five acres of Cabernet Sauvignon interspersed with Merlot, Malbec, Cabernet Franc and Petite Verdot.

Robert Sessions, winemaker since 1973, explains it is his intention "to maintain the highest quality possible in a chateau style operation." The stone winery is designed for efficiency and movement of the grapes. Grapes are harvested by hand, then brought to the winery where they are fermented in one-ton lots in 298 gallon, custom-made stainless steel fermenters.

Sessions points out that Chardonnay grapes are crushed and allowed to sit on the skins for a short time before pressing. The grapes are then fermented for eight to nine weeks at 55 degrees Fahrenheit, after which the wine is racked. "Our Chardonnay is aged for six to 12 months in 60 gallon Limousin oak barrels and one year in bottle," says Sessions.

The Pinot Noir, on the other hand, is crushed, destemmed and fermented to no color, then pressed. "The Pinot Noir gets two and a half years in wood and one to one and a half years in bottle," says Sessions.

Sessions reiterates the Hanzell philosophy that has been so well preserved through its succession of owners; "that everything should be done with care... following a Burgundian tradition of winemaking with liberal use of technology."

Valley of the Moon Winery

ESTATE BOTTLED
Valley of Moon
SONOMA VALLEY
FRENCH COLOMBARD
ALCOHOL 12% BY VOLUME
PRODUCED & BOTTLED BY
VALLEY OF THE MOON WINERY

Enrico and Harry Parducci have been the proud owners of the Valley of the Moon Winery & Vineyards since 1941. The concern is located on Madrone Road beside the Sonoma Creek in Glen Ellen, in the famous valley written about by author Jack London in his book, *The Valley of the Moon*.

The winery and vineyards have long been associated with proprietors and personalities who have helped to shape its history and establish its wines. Originally the land was part of the Agua Caliente Rancho and granted to Lazaro Pena as a gift from the Mexican government. Later M.G. Vallejo purchased the estate, and gave 640 acres of it to his children's piano teacher in exchange for lessons. In 1851, Joseph Hooker, of Union Army fame, bought the property and planted the first vineyard. However, it was owner George Whitman, who in 1876 produced the first 50,000 gallons of wine and 2,000 gallons of brandy.

In 1883, Eli T. Sheppard, former American consul to Tientsin, China, and later adviser to the Chinese Emperor on International law, acquired the land and called it Madrone Vineyards. He is responsible for planting French varieties and making the wines of the area so famous.

Multimillionaire mine owner and newspaper publisher United States Senator George Hearst (father of William Randolph Hearst) purchased the vineyards from Sheppard and invested large sums of money.

Planting the vineyard with the best Bordeaux varieties, he constructed two stone cellars with a capacity of 244,000 gallons.

In 1922, Louis Engelberg purchased the Madrone Vineyards. He operated the vineyards through the Prohibition and Depression years. Engelberg sold the grapes from his vineyards to other wineries, and maintained the high quality expected from Madrone Vineyards.

In 1941, Enrico Parducci, founder of the San Francisco Sausage Co., (now merchandised under the Columbus Brand label), bought Madrone Vineyards as a weekend retreat for his family and friends. Although grapes from the vineyards were sold commercially, the winery was in such a serious state of neglect that it wasn't until 1945 that it was renovated and the winery had its first crush. In that same year, Parducci embarked on a long-range program to replant the vineyards.

For nearly 30 years, Parducci worked to build a reputation and trade amongst restaurants and hotels throughout California, supplying them with jug wines such as Semillon, Claret, Burgundy, Zinfandel and Vin Rose, before his son Harry made a major policy change. Since the seventies, Valley of the Moon Winery has featured two separate, but distinct lines of wines: its 100 percent Sonoma Valley varietals grown from its own vineyards: French Colombard, Semillon, Zinfandel, Pinot Noir and Zinfandel Rose, and its California Private Stock jug wines.

"This winery has established its own taste," explains Harry Parducci, winemaker with Otto Toschi. "All I am trying to do is to produce good wine at a reasonable price that people can afford."

Grand Cru Vineyards

At the end of Vintage Lane in Glen Ellen, California, is Grand Cru Vineyards. It takes its name from the French appellation controllee designation literally meaning "great vineyards," but in fact designating the finest vintages.

The winery dates from 1970 when two engineering associates Robert Magnani and Allen Ferrara collaborated and built a winery by hand on the now rehabilitated stone foundations of the nearly 100-year-old Lamoine Cellars and the 30 acres of surrounding Zinfandel vineyards. The original owners had built an American version of a French chateau with a stately mansion and varietal vineyards. Magnani and Ferrera have built their idea of an American small estate.

The 20,000 case Grand Cru Vineyards produces an assortment of table wines (determined primarily by corporate contracts). They include 100 percent Sonoma County varietals (some of which bear a Sonoma Valley or Alexander Valley designation) such as Gewurztraminer, Chenin Blanc, Pinot Noir Blanc, Zinfandel and Cabernet Sauvignon. The whites are characteristically made in an off dry style (the exception being the new Sauvignon Blanc which will be fermented to dryness). The reds are traditionally dark, rich and full bodied, intended for five to 10 years bottle age.

Winemaker Magnani has made a name for Grand Cru Vineyards with his experimental and exotic bottlings. His dessert Gewurztraminer, a thick golden wine, lush on the palate, which sold for $17 a fifth, was an artificially induced wine from botrytis mold. His white Zinfandel was one of the first on the market made from ancient Zinfandel vines. He has also produced several Late Harvest type Zinfandels between 15-16.5 percent alcohol.

Since 1978, when Grand Cru Vineyards formed a limited partnership and several new investors came aboard, the management has made a critical assessment of its future production and direction. Major emphasis will focus on what Magnani describes as "Germanic style wines that are very fruity, aromatic, low in alcohol with a slight residual sugar."

New Sauvignon Blanc and Semillon plantings, the source of these new wines, will replace the old Zinfandel vineyards around the winery. Yolo County near Clarksburg supplies the Chenin Blanc (and is the one label that doesn't say Sonoma County). Garden Creek Ranch in the Alexander Valley is the site of the Cabernet Sauvignon, Pinot Noir and Gewurztraminer.

At this time, it is uncertain whether Grand Cru Vineyards will continue to make wine from all these grapes. "The spiraling cost of grapes such as Gewurztraminer," explains Magnani, "has caused us to look at the cold hard facts. We may have to severely limit Gewurztraminer production and make other wines because of economics."

The eighties also signify completion of a decade-long building program that includes the winery, vineyards and grounds. A new tasting room with an indoor fireplace and outdoor decks with arbors will overlook the fermentation chambers, new vineyards and picnic grounds.

Chateau St. Jean

Chateau St. Jean, one of the most spectacular new wineries in the Sonoma Valley, rests at the foot of Adobe Canyon in Kenwood, with Mt. Hood to the east and Sugarloaf Ridge to the west.

The extravagant Mediterranean complex was the dream of three men: Robert H. Merzoian, Edward L. Merzoian, Jr., and W. Kenneth Sheffield. It was founded in 1973 based on their commitment to produce superior quality wines from vineyards that are kept separate and bottled in small lots.

The Merzoian family, prominent San Joaquin Valley growers, designed their American wine estate on a European chateau concept, and called it Chateau St. Jean. Chateau was selected for its reference to the country castles and vineyard estates of France. Jean (which takes its pronunciation from the King's English) is for Jean Merzoian, one of the investor's spouse.

A splashing fountain dominates the central courtyard. Around the hillside and valley vineyards stands the chateau with its formal gardens of quince, fig, pomegranate, pine and palm and its small reflecting ponds simulating the Great Lakes. The winery building houses elaborate fermentation chambers, French wood aging cellars, corporate offices and a visitors center.

Chateau St. Jean hired Richard Arrowood, a graduate in chemistry from U.C. Sacramento, as winemaker with experience at F. Korbel Bros. and Sonoma Vineyards. Allan Hemphill, formerly vice president of operations at Korbel, was selected as president.

Primary emphasis is placed on white wine production from Chardonnay, Gewurztraminer, Johannisberg Riesling and Sauvignon Blanc. A very small amount of the production is devoted to Zinfandel, Cabernet Sauvignon and Merlot. The winery also makes small quantities of sparkling wines in the traditional methode champenoise.

Currently the winery draws 30 percent of its grape supply from the 135 acres of estate-grown grapes in and near the winery. The upper hillside vineyards, above the fog line, are excellent for Chardonnay, Sauvignon Blanc and Gewurztraminer. The lower valley vineyards, within the fog intrusion, are suitable for Johannisberg Riesling. The remaining 70 percent of the grapes are purchased from growers in Sonoma, Alexander and Napa Valleys. Formal studies have determined those vineyards best suited to a specific grape type; for example, Robert Young Vineyards produces quality Chardonnay; Glen Ellen Vineyards top Zinfandels and Wildwood Vineyards stately Cabernet Sauvignons.

Chateau St. Jean has impressed the public with its system of vineyard designating wines. In one vintage, the winery has produced seven different Chardonnays, eight different Johannisberg Rieslings (in a full range from Kabinnett to Trockenbeerenauslese), four Fume Blancs, two Gewurztraminers, two Zinfandels and four Cabernet Sauvignons. These wines range from a high of $40 for a Trockenbeerenauslese to $4.00 for the house wine.

Kenwood Vineyards

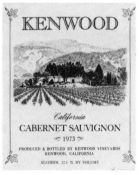

Kenwood Vineyards on Highway 12 in Kenwood has dedicated almost all of its future production to wines made from specific identified vineyards throughout the Sonoma Valley. Their dedication comes at a time when their own wines have gained recognition in the wine community, and their Sonoma Valley wine district is seriously threatened by development.

"It is in our interest and effort to emphasize local vineyards with a Sonoma appellation of origin," explains John Sheela, owner and president. "We want to be selective and designate only outstanding wines."

The Kenwood direction has evolved with thought, as well as trial and error. In 1970, a group of California wine enthusiasts—Martin Lee, his two sons, Michael and Martin, John Sheela, Neil Knott and their friend, Dr. Robert Kozlowski—formed a partnership to buy the Julius Pagani Winery along the Sugarloaf Ridge foothills. The concern had been in operation since 1906 as a bulk producer of red and white varieties, which were also marketed in half gallons under the Pagani label.

Upon the Pagani property were a wooded bungalow, several barns, a winery and wine equipment which the new owners put to use before they made capital intensive investments. During their first decade of operation, they bought grapes throughout Sonoma County and made a range of wines from the mid to premium varietals. Reds turned out to be their spe-cialty, and under the combined efforts of Dr. Kozlowski and Michael Lee, Kenwood Vineyards made itself a name.

In preparation for their second decade, the owners have made major policy as well as physical changes. Production will be limited to five noble varieties: Cabernet Sauvignon, Zinfandel and Chardonnay being of primary importance and Pinot Noir and White Riesling being of secondary importance. The winemakers will venture so far as to say they will produce Chardonnays and Cabernets from five different vineyards, and Zinfandels from several less, in one vintage year. Although this approach is still relatively new to the California industry, it is not without its considerations regarding time, detail, cost and consumer.

"Our red wines have always been in a range of drinkability," explains Sheels, "but our new wines are much more classic. All of a sudden people who are drinking our wines may be surprised by the change."

Kenwood has improved the existing grounds with the addition of turn-around driveway through the vineyards. Throughout the grounds there are floral gardens, stone terraces and charming walkways. Winery buildings are now equipped with new stainless steel jacketed fermenters, stainless steel storage tanks and hundreds of American and French oak barrels. A new warehouse building will consist of additional case storage, bottling line and business offices.

Sheela talks of the future with confidence. "We've stabilized our size, improved our grape source (20 acres of White Riesling exist on the property and 100 acres are under contract throughout Sonoma), and perfected individual batch fermentations in each cask and tank through all stages to bottle," he says.

Other Wineries

In the old stone Chauvet Winery on Arnold Drive in Glen Ellen is the firm of J.J. Haraszthy, great grandson and great, great grandson respectively of the famous Col. Agoston Haraszthy, was formed in 1977. Together they established the first wine blending venture of its type in the Sonoma Valley.

"I guess we both were inspired by the vision and energy that our forebear, Agoston Haraszthy, had for the California wine business," says Jan Haraszthy.

Yearly, outstanding lots of wine are purchased from wineries throughout California, then blended and finished by Val, winemaster, at the Glen Ellen facility. Special emphasis is placed on finding palatable dinner wines that can be sold under the J.J. Haraszthy label in the medium-price range.

The 3,000 case operation has limited quantities of vintage-dated premium, oak-aged varietals made of Zinfandel, Pinot Noir and Pinot Noir Blanc. All these wines are available in restaurants, wine shops and hotels throughout California.

"Our future plans are to expand our list," explains Jan, "and eventually work toward making our own wine."

KISTLER VINEYARDS

The Glen Ellen hills above the Sonoma Valley are the site of the 6,000 case Kistler Winery & Vineyards started by the Piedmont-based Kistler family in 1978.

Steve Kistler, who studied with Paul Draper at Ridge Vineyards in Cupertino is winemaker. Mark Bixler, former chemist from Fetzer Vineyards, holds the same title. John Kistler manages the vineyard.

"We looked for a year and a half at sites in Napa and Sonoma," says Bixler, "and felt growing conditions in the Sonoma Valley and the wines from local wineries most impressive."

The utilitarian hilltop winery, is designed with an underground cellars on one level and fermentation chambers, barrel aging and case storage on another level. Forty acres, at steep 1600 foot elevations, are planted to Cabernet Sauvignon, Pinot Noir and Chardonnay. The Chardonnays are barrel-fermented, and all the wines, including the Cabernet Sauvignon and Pinot Noir, are held by vineyard and so designated, with some oak, at prices from eight dollars a fifth.

Concludes Bixler, "We're looking forward to making some very exciting new wines."

VIEWS LAND COMPANY WINERY & VINEYARDS

The Views Land Company Winery and Vineyards dates from 1978 when Walter L. Bensen of Sonoma County decided to develop a winery and vineyard instead of houses.

Bensen proceeded with a 5,000 case premium winery located on Gehricke Road in Sonoma on a vineyard site that goes back to 1850. One Major Jacob C. Synder, past president of the Buena Vista Viticultural Society, had owned the land where the operation now stands.

Fifteen acres of valley and hillside along the foothills of the Mayacamas Mountains have been planted to Chardonnay and Gewurztraminer. Forty additional acres will be developed with the aforementioned varieties and Cabernet Sauvignon at another location.

Bensen, advised by a team consisting of MaryAnn Graf and Brad Webb, crushed his grapes and made wine for the first time in 1979. The new stone winery, with its underground cellars and sod roof, houses traditional fermentation equipment and a small French barrel cellar. The winery will produce Sonoma County premium varietals from Cabernet Sauvignon, Gewurztraminer and Chardonnay. Says Bensen, "The style of wine will be dictated by the characteristics of the grapes produced in the vineyard."

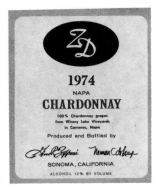

Z-D Winery was so named for its founders Gino Zepponi and Norman de Leuze. It started in a renovated barn on Burndale Road in Sonoma in 1969.

Since then, specialization has been focused on two Burgundian styled wines: Chardonnay and Pinot Noir. Z-D has long been noted as a pioneer in the California wine business for selecting vineyard sites in out-of-the-way growing areas throughout California. Some examples are the Rosa Vineyards in southern Napa County, the Rancho Tierra Vineyards near Paso Robles in San Luis Obispo, the Tori Beth Ranch in Carneros District and the Pickle Canyon Vineyards on Mt. Veeder in Napa County.

Besides the aforementioned wines, Z-D Winery makes a Riesling and Gewurztraminer, both sweet, and a full-bodied Zinfandel.

In 1979, Z-D Winery moved its facilities to a new location on the Silverado Trail in southern Napa Valley. Says Zepponi, winemaker with de Leuze, "We have always made natural wines. We age our wines in the same barrels in which they are made. As we virtually do nothing to the wine, they are totally natural."

California

Oregon

Nevada

Pacific Ocean

Arizona

Mexico

Central Sonoma County Wineries

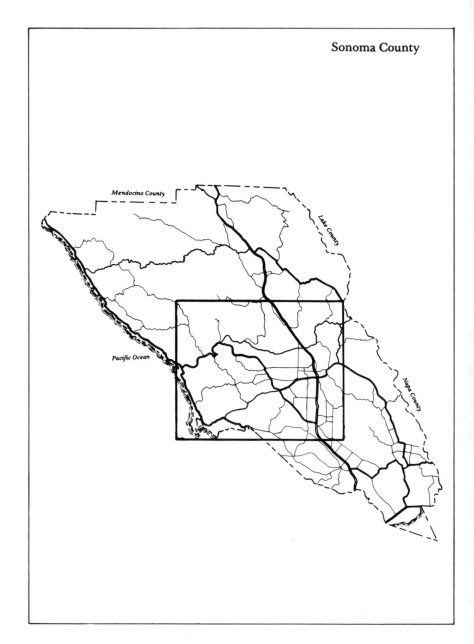

Sonoma County

Mendocino County

Lake County

Pacific Ocean

Napa County

Dehlinger Winery

Carole and Tom Dehlinger typify an up and coming generation of small winery operators who still believe in the merits of hard work to create a product of quality. They feature four vintage-dated Sonoma County varietals: Pinot Chardonnay, Cabernet Sauvignon, Pinot Noir and Zinfandel, which show promise for a winery so young. (It was founded in 1976).

For the Dehlingers the property adjacent to the Guerneville-Vine Hill crossroads had appeal for a number of reasons. Nearly a century earlier farmers had first cultivated the hills of Sebastopol, and discovered them to be perfect for orchards and vineyards. Besides the area's natural charm, the Dehlingers found the soils fertile and the cool nights and afternoon breezes irresistible.

"We came here because the climate was cooler than other areas, but still warm enough to grow grapes which ripen early," says Tom Dehlinger, winemaker and co-owner with his father Klaus Dehlinger. "I had witnessed damage to grapes due to high temperatures at other locales and wanted to try growing them in a cooler region."

Time spent at three prestigious wineries—Beringer Vineyards, Hanzell Vineyards and Dry Creek Vineyards—helped shape Dehlinger's approach to winemaking. He labels himself a traditionalist, and doesn't hesitate to point out the significance of details—"hand picking into lug boxes, fermenting in open redwood,

not filtering or fining and aging in oak." Dehlinger's education spans training at two of America's most advanced institutions—U.C. Berkeley and U.C. Davis —yet he holds steadfast to old, proven methodology.

Dehlinger espouses a straightforward, no-nonsense approach to his craft. "We make dinner wines meant to go with meals," he says, "nothing high in alcohol or dessert or late harvest in style."

Closer examination of his wines reveals a discernible style, a composite of grapes and technique. For now the majority of the grapes are purchased from other Sonoma County vineyardists, with a small percentage from the Dehlinger vineyards. In 1975 eight acres of Pinot Chardonnay, four acres of Pinot Noir and two acres of Cabernet Sauvignon were planted.

Dehlinger wines may accurately be described as Tom explains them—"big, heavy and substantial." Some of the wines carry this off with more finesse than others, but all of the wines are created in a style Dehlinger "conceives and likes." Clearly the Pinot Chardonnays and Cabernet Sauvignons were among the better examples of Dehlinger's capabilities. His Pinot Chardonnays tend to be fragrant, full, golden, dry wines. His Cabernet Sauvignons are rich, flavorful and powerful.

By comparison with other new wines tasted from the area, the Dehlingers have created some of the more adventuresome new wines to come out of Sonoma County. Collectively they have some very definite ideas. They have started a new winery in an area that hasn't produced fine wine for quite some time, and they have introduced their wines—good ones—with an established theme and marketable style.

Martini & Prati Wines, Inc.

High on top of Vine Hill in southern Sonoma County is Martini & Prati Wines, Inc. First known as the Lone Fir Vineyard, the business once belonged to Juliette and Joseph Atherton of Oahu, Hawaii, but it has been most closely associated over the years with the Martini name.

Before 1900, Rafaelo Martini from Lucca, Italy, voyaged around the Cape Horn to California. He prospered in agriculture and livestock in the Moss Beach-Princeton area. In 1902, he bought vineyards in Sonoma.

In 1910, son Narcisco Martini with some help from his five brothers bought out their father. They cleared more land and added other varietals, such as Zinfandel, to enlarge their line of bulk wines. The winery was the second largest firm in Sonoma County and it managed to function through Prohibition by making sacramental wines.

By 1943, the Martini property was sold to W.A. Taylor & Co., a subsidiary of the larger Hiram Walker & Co. Elmo Martini (now the oldest surviving family member) became manager of the former family operation and five other wineries in the Bay Area.

In 1951, Elmo Martini and Enrico Prati joined forces. They bought back the winery from Taylor and in the process created a historic merger of two noted California wine families. Prati had gained his professional experience first as a foreman then later as an owner of

Italian Swiss Colony. However, less than a year passed before Prati died and his son Edward assumed his position. Today, the winery is run by Elmo Martini, his two sons, Jim and Tom, and Edward (Pete) Prati, Jr.

Just off Laguna Road stands the winery landmark, a silver watertower which spells the winery's name in big, black letters. The ancient farmhouse sits behind the white, green-trimmed winery. The latter has seven gables and an overhanging ranch-style roofline.

"These two rows of 8,000 and 9,000 gallon redwood tanks, which I have moved three different times, were handmade around 1900," points out Martini. "They were lumbered at Guerneville and made expressly for the Trenton Winery (one of the old wineries in the area long since torn down).

The grapes are grown on the Martini farm and the Prati farm. The grapes consist of seven types of red and six types of white. Additional grapes are purchased from local growers. Martini and Prati sell the majority of their wine in bulk to Paul Masson and Gallo, but there is considerable production under the company label.

"At Martini & Prati, we make our wines in the Italian style. As with any winery, there are certain cellar characteristics or ways of treatment which are unique. As an example we make extensive use of redwood," says Martini.

As originally, the winery has been run primarily as a bulk operation with some interest in producing private labels for selected customers. Within the last 25 years, Martini & Prati put out a selection of dry table wines under their own label.

Joseph Swan Vineyards

1973
Sonoma

Estate **Pinot Noir** Bottled

Joseph Swan Vineyards

TABLE WINE 750 ML. (25.4 FL. OZ.)
Produced and Bottled by Joseph Swan Vineyards, Forestville, California

On the outskirts of Forestville near the Lagoon of the Roses is Joseph Swan Vineyards. It is situated at the intersection of Laguna and Trenton Roads in the heart of a very old grape and apple district.

Joseph Swan wines—his Zinfandel, Pinot Noir and Chardonnay (as available)—are among the most coveted wines in the American wine world. They are rich, aromatic, flavorful wines made in a classical Burgundian style.

The inspiration to make these wines came from books Joe read while a boy in South Dakota. Descriptions of wine so intrigued him that he concocted a brew of rhubarb wine in the upstairs attic and chicken coop that was unbeknownst to his teetotaler parents. Swan's passion for winemaking stayed with him throughout his flights in California as a pilot for Western Airlines and during his time off as well. One idea that captured his fancy was the establishment of a vitis vinifera vineyard of mixed varietals at 5,000 feet elevation in the Sierra Nevada in the sixties. Results from these blocks showed that Chardonnay and Pinot Noir would remain frost free.

The 13 acre vineyard estate where Swan resides in Santa Rosa dates from 1855 when it was used as the headquarters for the town of Trenton. The house was a combined grocery store, post office and switchboard for the community. Puncheons and casks found in the dirt cellar indicate the possible sale of wine sold by the jug at an earlier time.

Successive owners maintained orchards and vineyards on the property. When Swan bought the land in 1967, he acquired a pre-turn-of-the-century farmhouse, barn and a 60 year old Zinfandel vineyard. Swan proceeded to plant five acres of Chardonnay and five acres of Pinot Noir interspersed with some Cabernet Sauvignon. The majority of Swan's Zinfandel is purchased from growers in Sonoma and Mendocino Counties.

The winery officially dates from 1969 when it was bonded. Swan had already gained somewhat of a reputation in Sonoma for his production of Zinfandels of incredible intensity and proportion. One of his early Zinfandels was made from the old vines on the property. These grapes were fermented to extreme lengths of dryness on the stems, clarified with no filtering, then aged in French oak cooperage before extensive bottle age. Such was the style of his Zinfandels, and many of his Pinot Noirs to follow.

Joseph Swan Vineyards is a one-man operation dedicated to the principle of making good wine or none at all. The winery began simply in the cellar of Swan's house and over the years has been moved to the barn and a new cellar. All winemaking is done by hand from the selecting of the grapes to the tending of the wine. Emphasis is continually on letting the fruit speak in the character and taste of the wine.

You can't help but like Swan, a tall and stately man in his own right, with a striking shock of white hair, who when asked his specialty answers with elan, "My wines."

Mark West Vineyards

Mark West Vineyards

Anno 1976

Russian River Valley
Pinot Chardonnay

Produced, Cellared and Bottled by Mark West Vineyards
Forestville, Sonoma County, Calif.   Alcohol 12% by Vol.

Mark West Vineyards runs between the Trenton-Healdsburg Road and the Mark West Creek just outside of Forestville, California. The winery is named to honor the prominent Sonoma pioneer, Mark West, whose name can be found on buildings, roads and waterways throughout the county.

From 1972, when Connecticut-born tax specialist Joan Ellis and her husband Pan American pilot Robert Ellis first toured the Sonoma countryside, they were captured by its rural charms and intriguing contrasts to their home in the populated suburban Alamo.

A 116 acre dairy farm, with a roomy 1894 farmhouse and dairy barn, caught their fancy. They bought the property, and then proceeded to remodel the farmhouse, landscape the Japanese rose gardens and build a redwood winery.

For all intents and purposes the Ellises wished to be landowners, enjoying the country gentlepeople way of life. But, as so often happens to people who plant 62 acres of vineyards in the cooler coastal climes, varieties like Chardonnay, Gewurztraminer, Johannisberg Riesling and Pinot Noir, these grapes turn to wine. Mark West Vineyards is a case in point.

Joan Ellis (and Robert when his busy schedule allows it) became a winemaker out of necessity, not passion. "I always had a keen sense of taste," says Joan, "that must have developed out of all these cooking classes or merely a love for wine and food." Seizing the challenge, she enrolled at U.C. Davis in enology, taking the short course, followed by intensive summer study at Gisenheim Institute in Germany. When she came home for her first harvest in 1976, Lawrence Wara was there to advise her as consulting enologist. In 1979, her son Gary Atiaco, a former computer systems specialist, joined her, forming the only mother-son enological team in the West. Robert Ellis, co-owner with Joan, handles vineyard management, production and marketing.

"We're creating Mark West wines in two distinct regional European styles," says Joan, "from 100 percent California varietals."

The wines, handled in a typical Burgundian fashion, include the barrel-fermented Chardonnay, Pinot Noir and Gamay Beaujolais. All these wines are properly aged in barrel and bottle. Says Joan, "We're trying to create a Chardonnay, for example, that reflects oak that is carefully balanced with fruit."

The Johannisberg Riesling is made in a Late Harvest style whenever Botrytis cineria (noble rot) infects this hillside planted variety. The Gewurztraminer tends to be very Alsatian in style. "Our Gewurztraminer is spicy and off-dry, without being austere," says Joan.

The winery will be enlarged by 1980 to handle 20,000 cases a year. New offices, tasting room, fermentation area, oak cooperage and case storage will be developed. Future plantings of some 15 acres of Chardonnay will bring total acreage to 77.

F. Korbel & Bros.

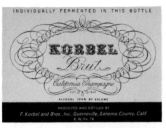

The red brick, ivy-laden Korbel Champagne Cellars & Vineyards overlook the banks of the Russian River in Guerneville (pronounced Gurnville), California. The winery represents the adventures and achievements of its Czechoslavakian founders the Korbel brothers: Francis, Anton and Joseph.

When the Korbels arrived in San Francisco from Prague in 1860, they found a burgeoning boomtown in need of skilled tradesmen and materials. Six thousand acres of redwood forest in Stumptown (later called Guerneville) were purchased by the brothers, much of the land for 35 cents an acre. When sources became depleted, and only stumps were to be found, the Korbels planted grapes for wine. European grape types thrived in this cool coastal climate.

The Korbels harvested their first grape crop in 1881, and due to a low grape price of $3.50 that year decided to crush grapes and make wine. The brick winery at Korbel dates from 1886. Brandymaking, however, commenced several years later in 1889 when a Norman tower and copper still were added to the facility.

By 1896 requests for champagne from San Francisco, then the entertainment capital of the West, caused the Korbels to ask Prague champagnemaster Frank Hazak to join them. He came to California and produced stunning dry sparkling wines. Hazek, and his successor Czech Jan Hanuska, popularized the Korbel name with their formulas for private cuvees.

Since 1954, the Heck family has owned Korbel Champagne Cellars. Adolf Heck, Champagne Master and President of Korbel studied champagnemaking at Gisenheim University in Germany, as a young man, then applied his skills working for his father at the Cook's Imperial Champagne in St. Louis. Later Adolf produced champagne for National Distillers in Ohio and came to California as President of Italian Swiss Colony in the early fifties.

Since their takeover of the business, the Hecks have put time, energy and money into an increasingly successful operation that emphasizes in order of importance champagne, brandy and wine. Increased champagne and brandy sales within the last three decades are cases in point. In the early sixties, Korbel produced just over 60,000 cases of champagne. Since that time sales have quadrupled. Brandy sales continue to increase with Korbel brandy rapidly becoming one of the most popular brandies produced in California.

These changes have not come without renovation and expansion. New production facilities have been added during the last 10 years. They consist of a champagne aging cellar, a new bottling line, a grape crushing plant and a new brandy operation. The modern brandy complex receives and bottles distilled brandy that comes from brandy distilleries in the San Joaquin Valley. The new production complex designed to cover future growth will be one of the most modern in the country set up to handle bottle-fermented champagne. This new facility will incorporate some new improvements such as an automated riddling system designed by Adolf Heck.

The Old Brandy Distillery at Korbel

The Korbel estate will be redesigned to better accommodate visitors to the old winery cellars. Korbel is remodeling their gift shop, landscaped gardens, picnic area and parking facilities. Restoration will be continued on many of the historic buildings at the winery. The brick brandy tower, railroad station, blacksmith shop, formal gardens and gazebo at the Korbel mansion will be opened to visitors in the near future. No cars will be allowed on the premises and all tours will be walking excursions.

Korbel has expanded its vineyards to 640 acres of vines along the Russian River. These vines are planted in Chardonnay, Johannisberg Riesling, Chenin Blanc, Gewurztraminer, Pinot Noir and Cabernet Sauvignon. Korbel is concentrating on estate-bottled wines from these vineyards.

Adolf L. Heck has reigned as President and Champagne Master since the Heck acquisition in the fifties. Jim Huntsinger, Korbel's winemaker and plant manager, joined the Korbel staff in 1970. Gary Heck, Adolf's son, is Executive Vice President and Manager. All of these men have witnessed great change in the Korbel champagne production.

Korbel champagnes are made in the classical French "methode champenoise," which requires secondary fermentation in the bottle. The primary fermentation duplicates the customary procedure for still wines, then the champagne cuvee is made from a blend composed of different vintages and varieties. Yeast and sugar are then added to the cuvee. This is bottled and the secondary fermentation begins. Yeast converts the sugar into alcohol and carbon dioxide.

Many months of aging with yeast and wine together produces champagne of superior quality.

Korbel ages its champagne for approximately two years on the yeast before they are placed on riddling racks. (This is the special machine invented at Korbel that shakes the bottles automatically and eliminates the traditional hand operation.) A portion of the wine is then disgorged to eliminate the yeast sediment. The lost wine is replaced and a dosage syrup is added. After recorking and securing the champagne with a wire hood, it is labeled and laid away for several months before it goes to the marketplace.

Korbel produces a bone dry Korbel Natural, an almost dry Korbel Brut, a semi-sweet Extra Dry, a sweet Sec, a dry Blanc de Noir and a semi-dry Sparkling Rose and Sparkling Rouge. Seventy percent of this champagne is sold out-of-state; the rest is sold locally.

Executive vice president Gary Heck, proud of Korbel's record to keep prices down and sales up, speaks of future growth based on American consumption patterns.

"We're just trying to make good champagne," explains Heck. "I look back four years ago when wine was $2.25 a bottle and our champagne was priced in the $7.00 range. Wine has since quadrupled in price on most restaurant wine lists, but our prices have stayed in the $8.00 category."

The Korbel Champagne Cellars has to be one of the more exciting stories to come out of Sonoma County. The importance of this champagne and brandy operation is only now being felt, and will make an intense impact on the American consumer in the future.

Davis Bynum Winery

In 1964 Davis Bynum made a major decision which changed his life. He left his job as a reporter for the San Francisco Chronicle and became a California winemaker. One year later, in 1965, he founded and opened the Davis Bynum Winery in Albany, California, not far from the campus of the University of California in Berkeley.

Bynum began his wine efforts by buying bulk wine which he blended and bottled under his own label. In 1971, he purchased a 25-acre vineyard in the Napa Valley, from which he obtained grapes for making wine at the Albany Winery. The winery gained public attention for its whimsical Barefoot Bynum label, fondly called the Chateau La Feet of California; for its Mead, made from natural honey, and for its Davis Bynum line of dry table wines.

In 1973, as business improved, the Davis Bynum Winery, Inc. was formed and its owners purchased the 82-acre River Bend Ranch near the Russian River in Healdsburg. The Albany Winery was then closed in 1976.

The property of the new ranch was formerly the site of a prosperous hops ranch whose beginnings dated to the early 1900s. In 1949, the first hop kiln on the property had burned to the ground, but was reconstructed soon after. The second hop kiln is the present day Davis Bynum Winery.

As an individual Davis Bynum is a very warm and kind person. A fourth generation Californian, he was greatly influenced in his winemaking endeavors by his father, Lindley Bynum, an historian and wine judge who wrote *California Wines and How to Enjoy Them.* Today, Bynum has successfully realized his dream of growing grapes and making wine in Sonoma County.

Approximately 85 percent of the winery's grapes are grown by shareholders in vineyards along or near Westside Road in Healdsburg. Included are 20 acres of Pinot Noir and 25 acres of Chardonnay. The vineyards are planted on hills and benchland to take advantage of the southeastern exposure. In addition, the presence of the Russian River accounts for cooler weather and some fog, which results in an extended ripening period.

"Our concept is to concentrate on Sonoma County," explains Bynum with a smile. "We want to define specific areas in which grapes can be grown such as Zinfandel from the Dry Creek Valley or Pinot Noir from Westside Road."

As winemaker Bynum believes in making and holding the majority of his white wines in stainless steel, resulting in the production of fresh, young, fruity wines. The one exception to this rule is his Chardonnay, which is aged in wood and bottle for added complexity and character. All the red wines are aged in a combination of French, American and Yugoslavian oak with additional time in bottle before release.

Until very recently the winery has offered small lots of many different varietals. With the 1978 vintage, however, production has been limited to Chardonnay, Fume Blanc, Cabernet Sauvignon, Pinot Noir and Zinfandel. A Sonoma Red and a Sonoma White are now available.

Hop Kiln Winery

Russian River Valley
French Colombard
Alcohol 12.3% by volume

Produced and bottled by the Hop Kiln Winery
at Griffin Vineyard, Sonoma County, Healdsburg, California

The imposing stone and redwood turreted Hop Kiln Winery in Healdburg is a California Historic Landmark and National Trust building in honor of Sonoma County's former hopgrowing industry. The winery and vineyards are located at the bend of Westwide Road, just beyond the turn-off to Sweetwater Springs.

Dr. L. Martin Griffin, the Public Health Officer at Sonoma State Hospital, started to make wine as a hobbyist from grapes growing on his Sweetwater Springs Ranch, bought in 1961. The ranch formerly belonged to Solomon Walters who had a large scale hop production, a key ingredient for making beer, and dates from 1905. From 1975, when the winery was bonded, Dr. Griffin has made wines. The winery is a family enterprise with Dr. Griffin's daughter Carol and her husband John Warne heading tasting and sales.

"We use our own grapes to our best advantage," says Griffin, founder of the Audubon Canyon Ranch in Bolinas, "and make premium wines as naturally as possible."

The 65 acres of terraced, hillside vineyards are situated above the Russian River Valley. There are 20 acres of Petite Sirah and Zinfandel planted in the 1880's; 12 acres of Johannisberg Riesling, 15 acres of French Colombard and five acres each of Chardonnay, Gewurztraminer and Gamay Beaujolais planted in the past two decades. "Several microclimates throughout our vineyards permit us to plant almost any grape type," says Carol.

Studies in winemaking in France, Italy and Germany gave Dr. Griffin the background to set up his estate-bottled, 100 percent varietal, Russian River appellation wine program with the aforementioned varieties. Two wines have gained notoriety for their blend as well as their names. "A Thousand Flowers" is an estate wine made in a dry Alsatian style from French Colombard and Johannisberg Riesling. "Marty Griffin's Big Red," again an estate blend, is a flavorful mixture of grapes from the pre-turn-of-the-century vineyard of Zinfandel, Petite Sirah and Early Burgundy. Unusual vineyard conditions causing Botrytis Cinerea or "noble rot," have produced a spaetlese, auslese and trochenbeerenauslese style of wines. The latter is called "Weihnachten," a Johannisberg Riesling.

The Hop Kiln Winery is almost completely restored and equipped. Already Dr. Griffin has restored the ridge pole connecting the two major sections of the winery and rebuilt the fallen tower. An upstairs tasting room includes a museum with views of the limestone kilns, the furnace and the two-story hop press, as well as artifacts and tools. The winery itself has been outfitted with a crushing pad, stemmer-crusher, stainless steel fermenting tanks, two new 1200 gallon upright oak tanks and an improved labeling and bottling line.

"As a winemaker, I let the seasons work for me," says Dr. Griffin. "I let the cold winter do the precipitating and the fining. I keep the winery cold. By careful tending, the wine clears up naturally with minimal mechanical interference."

Mill Creek Winery

Mill Creek Vineyards is a small family owned and operated winery on the Westside Road near Healdsburg. It is managed by two enterprising brothers, Robert (Bob) Kreck, who handles winemaking, and William (Bill) Kreck, who oversees vineyard management.

Dry Creek Valley dry table wines produced from the most noble red varieties —Cabernet Sauvignon, Pinot Noir and Merlot—and one white variety, Chardonnay, are their "grown, produced and bottled estate specialties." Hearty full-bodied Cabernet Sauvignons are blended with Merlot and aged in a combination of French and American oak to achieve a wine to accompany meats and stews. Other variations on this same grape type are a tart, medium-bodied rose, Cabernet Blush (named in a moment of whimsy by wine columnist Jerry Mead and thus trademarked by the winery) and a blanc-styled Cabernet Gold for summer chilling. Pinot Noir is offered two ways, as a heavy dinner wine, and again as a blanc-type Pinot Noir called Burgundy Blanc for an aperitif with lighter menus. The dry Chardonnay stands well alone, or with fish, chicken or boullabaise.

Since 1949, when transplanted southern Californians Vera and Charles Kreck came to Sonoma (when land prices were reasonable and farming their life), they devoted their mutual interests to ranching and cattle raising in the Mill Creek watershed west of Healdsburg. Beginning in 1965, the Krecks established 65 acres of vines, primarily Cabernet Sauvignon, with some Pinot Noir, Chardonnay and Merlot, at the southern end of the Dry Creek Valley. They named their property Mill Creek Vineyards after the family homestead, some 20 years old, four miles from the vineyard.

The Krecks began by growing grapes which they sold commercially, and gradually the love of wine prompted them to start a winery. The first two crushes, in 1974 and 1975, were at other wineries while the Krecks converted an existing building to a winery. In 1976, the winery was officially bonded and the first wines released to the public. "It has always been our intention to produce fine table wines from the grapes we grow," says Kreck, "and sell the wines at a reasonable price." This wise approach has been the backbone of the family's sales effort to restaurateurs and retailers throughout the country.

A beautiful, flower-filled garden and tree-lined avenue mark the approach to Mill Creek Vineyards. The winery is designed in two parts. The upper hillside cellar, a 6,000 square foot converted dairy barn, contains the stainless steel fermentation chambers and Yugoslavian, French and American oak aging cellars. The lower valley section, recently enlarged to 4,000 square feet, houses business and sales offices, a new modern bottling and labeling line and case storage.

The future of this family enterprise is to make its name with its established theme of good, medium-priced table wines from important red varieties before, with or after the dinner meal.

79

Landmark Vineyards

LANDMARK

SONOMA VALLEY

CHARDONNAY
1974

Alcohol 13.4% by volume
Produced and Bottled by the Cellars of Landmark Vineyards, Napa, California

An avenue of tall and stately cypress, over 100 years old, graces the entrance to one of Windsor, California's smaller family owned and operated wineries, Landmark Vineyards.

Founded in 1974 as the joint venture of William Mabry, Jr., his wife Maxine, their son, William Mabry, III, and daughter-in-law Michele, the project was conceived on this simple, but honest philosophy: "to make the best possible wines at the fairest prices."

"To meet this end," says Mabry, III, winemaker, "we've planted our own vineyards so that we can supervise them; we've remained small so that I can personally control the vineyard operation and we've done as much work as possible ourselves to keep costs down."

The Mabrys, residents of the county who were familiar with the wine business long before they got into it, grew grapes and made wine on a small ranch near Sonoma in the early seventies. By 1974, they took possession of the 77 acre Windsor estate, now known as Landmark's Home Ranch, as the site of their wine operation.

"We were intrigued with the property," remarks Michele, chief administrator, "because the ranch had been used for agricultural purposes since its inception. The soils were good and the climate ideal for our white varieties."

Early histories trace use of the ranch back to the 1800's when it was utilized as a site for branding cattle; during the 1900's it was a prune operation with orchards and dryers. The rambling Spanish hacienda, with its formal gardens, wooded glens and reflecting pool, were easily converted into an attractive sales and tasting room. Adjacent to the hacienda, Mabry, Jr., a retired Air Force officer and architect, designed a Spanish style winery with stucco walls, shake roof and arched doors; Mabry, III, and carpenter friend, Ronald Luddy, constructed it.

"In the past we've made wine from our own vineyards," says Michele, pointing out that in 1978 Landmark built a new wing to the winery and expanded to 10,000 cases, "but today our vineyards can't keep up with our growth so we produce and contract grapes from Sonoma and Napa."

There are three primary areas where Landmark Vineyards has its own grapes: 60 acres in the Alexander Valley are planted in Cabernet Sauvignon, Pinot Noir and Chardonnay; 17 acres in the Sonoma Valley are planted in Chardonnay and Pinot Noir; and 10 acres at the Home Ranch are planted half in Gewurztraminer and half in Johannisberg Riesling. "We have an additional 50 acres left to plant on our Home Ranch," says Michele, "and hope to see this accomplished by 1980."

Landmark Vineyards prides itself in making wines of good quality that are priced between $4.25 and $7.00. "It's getting to the point," says Michele, "where the consumer can't afford to pay $9.00 for Chardonnay. We're just trying to produce the best possible, full-bodied dry table wines, without charging an arm and a leg."

Sonoma Vineyards

Along the Old Redwood Highway in Windsor is the spectacular, multi-million dollar Windsor Winery at Sonoma Vineyards. This 20th century extravaganza, with its maltese cross-designed winery, splashing fountains and outdoor Greek amphitheatre, was the vision of Rodney D. Strong. This one-time international dancer-turned choreographer began his second career driven by the desire to master wine as he had dance.

Sonoma Vineyards wines made their debut in 1959 under the Tiburon Vintners label, product of a small cottage industry started by Strong in the seaside Tiburon, California. Wines were bought, blended and bottled, then sold at retail from the Victorian headquarters on Main Street. "It was a typical European arrangement," recalls Strong, "with a living quarters upstairs, wine shop downstairs and winery in the cellar."

Soon, Strong was in the mail order business shipping wines throughout California. Then, in a moment of genius, he thought to personalize his labels with catchy sayings and greetings that enraptured the public. What started as a one-man business mushroomed into a multi-million dollar enterprise.

Two years later, Strong rented the Windsor Winery, 60 miles north of Tiburon in the Russian River Valley. In 1962, the winery was purchased and plans were made for national distribution. Peter Freidman,

advertising executive from Doyle, Dane & Bernbach in New York, joined Strong in 1964. When the 50,000 case capacity Windsor Winery could no longer satisfy demand, plans were made to construct a 3 million gallon winery and vineyards.

Windsor Winery was renamed Sonoma Vineyards and opened at its present site in 1971. Sales continued to increase as Sonoma Vineyards went public (one of the first wineries in the state) and stock skyrocketed. In the mid-seventies, however, the winery ran into difficulties when they couldn't crack the national market.

Today Sonoma Vineyards has survived this growth cycle and approaches the 80's on the skill of Strong's winemaking and the corporate wisdom of Kenneth J. Kwit, board chairman, John W. Anderson, president and Alin Gruber, vice president, who purchased Sonoma Vineyards in conjunction with the national marketing agents Renfield Importers of New York in 1975.

Sonoma Vineyards continues to produce two separate, but distinct, lines of table wines, featuring varietals, generics, sparkling and dessert wines from the 1,398 acres of estate vines. The jewels of the Sonoma Vineyards, vineyard-designate line are the Chalk Hill and River West Chardonnays, River West Zinfandels, River West Pinot Noirs, Alexander's Crown Cabernet Sauvignons and River West, Le Baron, Late Harvest Johannisberg Rieslings. The recently introduced Sonoma Table Wines come in a dry white, red and rose. The Brut Champagne, made at the Windsor Winery Champagne Cellars, is one of the top three fermented-in-the-bottle champagnes in the state.

Foppiano Vineyards

Foppiano
Vineyards

RUSSIAN RIVER VALLEY

CABERNET SAUVIGNON

ALCOHOL 12% BY VOLUME
PRODUCED AND BOTTLED BY L. FOPPIANO WINE CO.
HEALDSBURG / SONOMA COUNTY / CALIFORNIA

Four generations of Foppiano family have worked to build Foppiano Vineyards into a national name. "We've blazed the way into the nation's wine markets twice," says Louis M. Foppiano, a great grandson of the founder. "After repeal of Prohibition my Father (Louis J. Foppiano) started bottling for eastern distribution, and for many years we were the second largest bottling winery in Sonoma County."

Now, with concentration on vintage-dated varietals, the Foppiano name is repeating a pattern started so many years ago. The winery and vineyards which produce these Sonoma County wines are located along the eastern border of the Russian River just south of Healdsburg. The almost perfectly square 200 acres of vines are part of the old Mexican Sotoyome land grant.

John Foppiano, founder of Foppiano Vineyards, came to California from Italy in the late 1800s, lured by talk of riches in the gold mines of Sonora, California. Although unsuccessful in his mining ventures, Foppiano was successful in discovering the fertile agricultural preserve along the Russian River. Starting with vegetables and orchards, his common sense soon told him there was greater opportunity in vines and grapes. In 1896, he bought a working winery and residence (the old Riverside Inn) and one year later founded the Foppiano Wine Co.

The early days were not without struggle. The family worked from dawn until dusk, slowly building a clientele and reputation. In 1910, Louis Andrew Foppiano was in a position to buy the bulk winery from his father. Following his death, and in accommodation to Prohibition, son Louis Joseph Foppiano and his widow Mathilda rebuilt the winery and broadened distribution. Tourists to the area carried the wines home and spread the word about Foppiano generics. With the boom of the sixties, the Foppianos joined the trend towards varietals and increased production.

By 1979, production had increased to 200,000 cases annually, following renovation and expansion of the facilities. The main winery was transformed into a storage area with redwood tanks and stainless storage. New stainless steel fermentation tanks were installed, and hundreds of American oak barrels were added to the cooperage.

Foppiano Vineyards produces vintage-dated Sonoma County wines (some with a Russian River Valley designation) from estate grown grapes and local growers' grapes. These wines include Cabernet Sauvignon, Pinot Noir, Petite Sirah, Zinfandel, Chardonnay, Sonoma Fume, Chenin Blanc and French Colombard. Today 60 percent of the production is in whites and 40 percent is in reds.

Rod Foppiano, also great grandson of the founder, joined his father and brother in 1972 following graduation from Fresno State with a degree in viticulture. He has taken great strides to upgrade the Foppiano line, especially the whites, and produce wines with more character and content.

Sotoyome Winery

It wasn't until William Chaikin, a Los Angeles manufacturer, and John Stampfl, a printer, collaborated and started a small northern California winery in 1973 that the name "Sotoyome" came into commercial existence.

Sotoyome Winery is named for the Mexican land grant upon which the vineyards and winery are situated. It is said that the name means "village of brave warriors," referring to the band of Indians who inhabited the nearby Russian River Valley.

The Chaikin-Stampfl alliance began as hobby which developed into a secondary profession. The project was mapped out with thought to a proven location with a historical grape past. The ranch of Anacleto Ricci, a prosperous fruit farmer, was chosen because of its position in a fertile agricultural belt of vineyards and orchards that had been developed by French and Italian crop farmers.

A panoramic hilltop off Limerick Lane in Healdsburg is the site of the redwood house and metal winery. For several years Chaikin and Stampfl experimented with several varieties before they refined their line to four grape types: Cabernet Sauvignon, Zinfandel, Petite Sirah and Chardonnay.

Now, the Petite Sirah and Zinfandel come from vines within the vicinity of the winery. (The 65 year old Zinfandel vines on the property, used to make that wine, will shortly be torn out and replaced.) The Cabernet Sauvignon and Chardonnay originate from Dry Creek Valley vineyards.

Chaikin endorses the Russian River Valley as an excellent area for grapes. "The mornings are frequently foggy with a slow accumulation of daytime, hillside heat," he says. "In the flat of the valley high temperatures are reached by mid-morning. The combination of the ever-changing Russian River watercourse and natural earthquake faults have produced fertile soils for grapes high in acid with good color and plenty of sugar."

Serving as winemaker, Stampfl, a graduate of U.C. Davis with a degree in enology and viticulture, has grown grapes and made wine in the Sonoma area for 30 years. At Sotoyome Winery he places importance on "a natural means of winemaking with as little manipulation and complication of the process as possible."

Wines are made in quantities of less than 4,000 cases annually in the efficient two-man winery which is equipped with glass lined storage tanks, stainless steel jacketed fermenters and small American oak cooperage. The owners have improved the facilities for tasting and retail sales, as well as increased their supply of American barrels.

"The biggest change," explains Chaikin, who has established local markets and gained some exposure in Colorado and Texas, "is our barrel storage capability. Normally all our red wines are released after a minimum of two years while our white wine is released after one year."

Cambiaso Winery and Vineyards

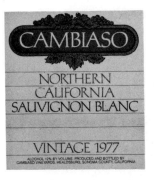

CAMBIASO

NORTHERN
CALIFORNIA
SAUVIGNON BLANC

VINTAGE 1977

ALCOHOL 12% BY VOLUME. PRODUCED AND BOTTLED BY
CAMBIASO VINEYARDS, HEALDSBURG, SONOMA COUNTY, CALIFORNIA

Cambiaso Winery and Vineyards are situated in the hillside wine district to the southeast of Healdsburg overlooking the Russian River Valley. The winery was founded in 1934 by Maria and Giovanni Cambiaso, a determined Italian couple who left San Francisco for the warmer climate and agricultural opportunities of Sonoma County.

By working for Italian neighbors in Healdsburg, they were able to earn enough money to buy a 52 acre ranch. Daughter Rita Cambiaso recalls stories of how hard her parents worked to clear the land of its native field stone to plant a Carignane vineyard and build a house and barn. "Times weren't all that easy," she recalls, "and sacrifices had to be made before my parents could enjoy their successes."

Cambiaso Winery developed its reputation on a universal theme of friendship, goodwill and service. These traditions evolved out of the practices of Giovanni Cambiaso, who loved people as he did wine. "My father always made a special point of placing the customer first," remarks Cambiaso. Giovanni evinced his appreciation of his neighbors, ranchers and patrons by personally delivering grapes (the sale of which were the initial means of raising investment capital for the winery building) direct to the consumer. This tradition has been translated into the more contemporary policy

"to make wine that everyone can enjoy."

The Cambiaso name has long been associated with restaurateurs and retailers who needed good wine provided in gallon or barrel quantities. "We're one of the old Italian wineries founded in the thirties," says winemaker Robert Fredson, fourth generation of a well known wine family from the Dry Creek Valley, "that still provides wines to restaurants in quantities (now litre sizes) the way we used to."

Since 1972, Cambiaso Winery has been owned by the wealthy Thailand distillers belonging to the Likit-prakong family, who do business in the United States as the Four Seas Corporation. Since the change in ownership, huge investments have been made in the building of new winery facilities, with installation of temperature-controlled stainless steel jacketed fermenters and additional warehouse and storage areas. Annual production has increased from 150,000 gallons to 750,000 gallons annually. "We're producing about 80,000 cases of wine a year," comments Fredson.

Cambiaso Winery now makes wine under two commercial labels: its vintage-dated, Northern California premium varietals such as Cabernet Sauvignon, Petite Sirah, Zinfandel, Chenin Blanc and Sauvignon Blanc and its 1852 House line which features a Burgundy, Chablis and Rose. The aforementioned wines derived their name from the handcrafted wines that Giovanni Cambiaso used to sell door to door to his neighbors in Healdsburg. Grapes for these wines are obtained from the 35 acres of vines at the winery, and from growers throughout California.

Other Wineries

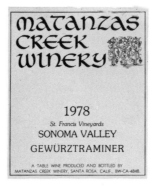

Iron Horse Ranch & Vineyards, one of the newest premium wineries in Sonoma County, lies in the western foothills of Sebastopol between the Sonoma Coast and the Santa Rosa Plains. Barry Sterling, international lawyer, and his wife Audrey, present owners, conceived their wine estate while living in France in the seventies. The Sterlings, who purchased 250 acres in the mid-seventies, have painstakingly brought historic detail and artistic authenticity to what promises to be a Burgundian approach to winemaking with some latitude for improvisation.

The Iron Horse Vineyards consist of 110 acres of half Chardonnay and Pinot Noir. The T Vineyards, some 40 acres owned by Forest and Kate Tancer of the Alexander Valley, will supply Sauvignon Blanc, Zinfandel and Cabernet Sauvignon.

The first wines were crushed in the barn-style turn of the century winery in the fall of 1979. Six thousand cases of Chardonnay, Pinot Noir and Cabernet Sauvignon were produced. By 1985, production will be increased to 25,000 cases, when all vineyards are fully bearing fruit.

"I think in growing and creating a product," says Audrey Sterling, "that you can find a passion for that project which is constantly changing in complexion and commitment."

Matanzas Creek is the only wine establishment to develop vineyards and winery in the pastoral Bennett Valley, due east of the Santa Rosa Plains.

Owners Sandra and David Steiner, explored the area in 1971 and were intrigued by growing grapes at the foot of the Sonoma Mountain. Winemaker Merry Edwards, formerly of Mt. Eden, had worked with grapes from Sonoma and liked the area for its "cooler climates and diverse microclimates." "When you come to a new district," she says, "vines are often younger and you have to let the wine guide you."

Matanzas Creek Vineyards are situated to take advantage of two contrasting microclimates. Cabernet Sauvignon is grown below the mountain but above the fog line. Chardonnay and Merlot are in the valley where the fog breaks. "I have a policy of waiting until the grapes are extremely ripe before we pick them," says Edwards. "There is nothing fancy that I do, it's just watching out over the process."

But fancy or not the new wines from this winery promise to be first rate. Although their list is by no means complete, Edwards is dedicated to production of three estate-grown, 100 percent varietals from Cabernet Sauvignon, Merlot and Chardonnay. Experimentation is also being done with Pinot Noir, Gewurztraminer, Semillon, Sauvignon Blanc and Pinot Noir Blanc.

Berle Beliz was a chemical engineer at the Livermore Radiation Laboratory before he founded the Willowside Vineyards in Santa Rosa. He had to drink lots of bad wine before he came across the Burgundies and Bordeaux that convinced him how really good wine should taste.

In 1970, quite by accident, he purchased Sonoma real estate with a farmhouse, winery and vineyard upon it. To the ten acres of 50-year-old Zinfandel vines he added Chardonnay, Gewurztraminer, White Riesling and Pinot Noir. From these grapes, which he enjoyed farming, he made his first home wines.

In 1975 he established a commercial winery venture in partnership with several vineyard growers who supplied him with quality grapes. "My basic approach is to keep each batch by vineyard separate, making several examples of the wines in which we specialize: Zinfandel, Pinot Noir, Chardonnay and Gewurztraminer," explains Beliz.

Today the 7,000 case Willowside Vineyards produces regional vineyard wines from 100 percent of the variety so named from sites like Chalk Hill, Lytton Springs, and Mt. Olivet. Future plans are to build a new winery within the Alexander Valley.

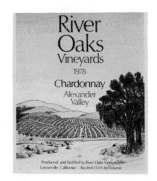

There is no doubt that the River Oaks Vineyards wine concept has to be one of the most innovative approaches to creating and marketing premium varietal wines from choice North Coast varietals for under $5.00 a bottle.

River Oaks Vineyards has built an appealing wine image based on a carefully constructed plan. Grapes for wine come from some 1,000 acres of vines in the Alexander and Dry Creek Valleys developed by owners of the Breckenridge Colorado Ski Resort. Finished wines are made at cooperative winery sites throughout Sonoma County, then cellared at various warehouses in California.

"Our policy is to produce 100 percent varietals from quality grapes grown in our vineyards for under $5.00 a bottle. We feel we've found the spot that produces grapes of high intensity and varietal flavor," says Frank Woods, Chairman of the Board.

River Oaks Vineyards produces nationally distributed premium vintaged, estate, Alexander and Dry Creek Valley appellation wines from Pinot Chardonnay, Cabernet Sauvignon, Pinot Noir, Zinfandel, Johannisberg Riesling. A gimmicky Soft Zinfandel and a slide-down-the-throat Gamay Beaujolais are particularly successful.

California

Oregon

Nevada

Pacific Ocean

Arizona

Mexico

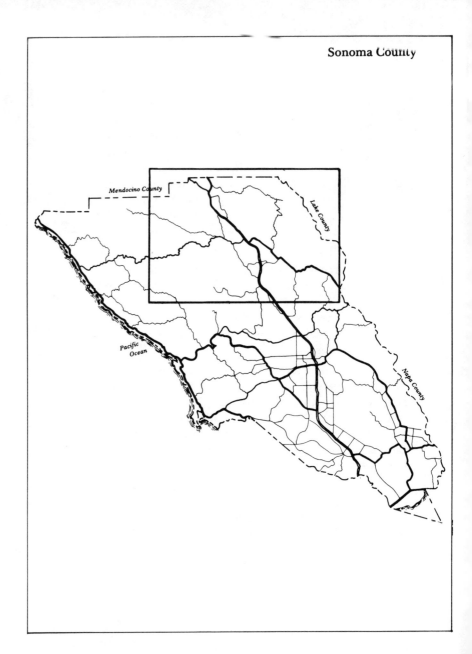

Sonoma County

Mendocino County

Lake County

Pacific Ocean

Napa County

Northern Sonoma Wineries

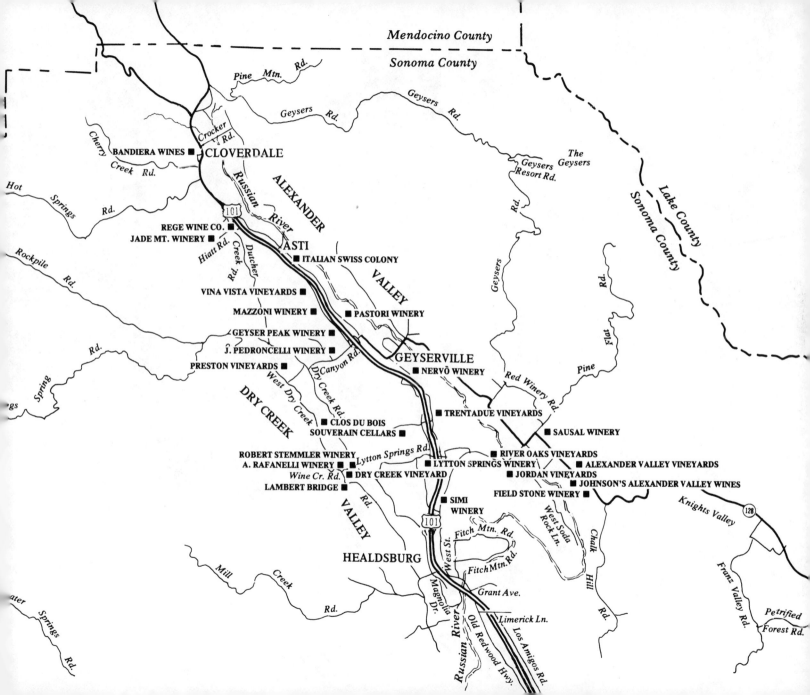

Dry Creek Vineyard

Seventy miles north of San Francisco lies a 100-year-old grape district known as the Dry Creek Valley. It was to this valley that former Bostonian David S. Stare came to start a small premium winery.

Stare's wine appreciation developed while a student at Massachusetts Institute of Technology, but his decision to enter the wine business as a professional didn't occur until after he had visited France in the seventies. Upon his return from Europe he enrolled in U.C. Davis to study viticulture and enology before buying his ranch in 1972. Since then, Dry Creek Vineyards has built a following as a pioneer small winery which makes premium table wines almost exclusively from the Dry Creek Valley.

Around the ivy-covered stone winery are 50 acres of vines. There are 10 acres each of Fume Blanc, Chenin Blanc and Cabernet Sauvignon and 20 acres of Chardonnay. These wines were first harvested in 1976, and when they fully mature will supply over half the winery's production. Currently growers in Dry Creek and Alexander Valley provide two-thirds of the grapes used.

Dry Creek Vineyards produces vintage-dated wines (many of which feature a Dry Creek or Sonoma County appellation of origin) in case lots of Chardonnay, Fume Blanc, Chenin Blanc, Zinfandel, Petite Sirah, Cabernet Sauvignon and Rose of Cabernet. Merlot and Gewurztraminer are sometimes available as will be future bottlings of Special Selection Cabernet Sauvignon to be bottle aged at the winery.

The Rose of Cabernet Sauvignon and the Chenin Blanc are for current consumption, and contain a small amount of residual sugar, but they are nevertheless considered dry. All the other wines are totally dry (except the sweeter style Gewurztraminer) and age well. The wines as a collection represent a level of "winemanship" that places this winery at the top.

When Stare started his project he admits he had but one long-term goal in mind: "to make top quality wines from the Healdsburg area." He has equipped his winery and practiced techniques which are compatible with this philosophy. Fume Blancs and Chenin Blancs, for example, are cold-fermented in stainless steel to ensure freshness and the slightly acidic finish typical of the winery's style. Chardonnays are fermented in a combination of stainless steel and oak cooperage for a more complex Burgundian composition. Cabernets, Zinfandels and Petite Sirahs, typically rich and round, are made very traditionally but in a more readily drinkable style. All these wines undergo the "bare minimum of fining and filtering as these processes remove many components that go into fine wine."

Varietal juice from different local growers is kept separate and stored this way until Stare decides on the final blend. "There is a very subjective feeling about what goes together," explains Stare, "and the final blend really lies in the taste."

Lambert Bridge

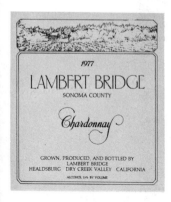

Jerry and Margaret Lambert are the proud owners of Lambert Bridge Winery in the Dry Creek Valley. They are yet another example of the new breed of entrepreneur dedicated to the production of quality wines and the preservation of an important wine district.

"I want to make the best wines at the most reasonable cost," says Lambert whose first released 1976 Sonoma County Chardonnay, priced at $6.50 a bottle, sold out in less than a month in major California retail wine shops. "I don't think pricing should be based on what the market bears. Price should be based on the value of the wine."

In 1970, the Lamberts embarked on an energetic program of developing their vineyards, some 80 acres: 22 acres of Chardonnay; 18 acres of Cabernet Sauvignon; 12 acres of Pinot Noir; and 10 acres of Johannisberg Riesling. "I can't stress enough the importance of soil," comments Lambert, "wine is made in the vineyard."

The Dry Creek Valley is an unusual, self-contained geographical entity which for years produced fine growing grapes, but only within the last decade has produced such outstanding wines. Winemaker Nick Martin, who shares Lambert's philosophy, explains, "We worked hard to grow grapes in the heart of the valley to take advantage of the deep and rich Yolo loams." Adds general manager Dave Rafanelli, whose ancestors have cultivated these soils for years, "There is no doubt about it...the Dry Creek soils produce strong, flavorful, regional wines."

It wasn't until 1975, after Lambert had witnessed several successful harvests from his vineyards, that he considered building a winery. "When I grew grapes," he explains, "it seemed that to sell them took away from growing them..." So, he found an architect to construct a modern California structure made of massive redwood timbers and beams inside and outside. "The winery was designed to blend in with the landscape," points out Martin. When the winery was named, it was merely a coincidence that it had the same name as the owner. Says Martin, "the facility was placed with a view of the Lambert Bridge in mind."

Great attention has been paid to equipping the facility properly—Demoisey crusher, Vaslin press and 135 gallon French Limousin oak puncheons. "What we're after," says Lambert, "is to derive 100 percent essence of the variety." One technique the winemaker practices to achieve this end is to ferment totally in puncheons. Martin adds, "We want to leave the character of the grape in the wine, so we do minimal processing."

Lambert Bridge produces two estate, vintaged wines: Cabernet Sauvignon and Chardonnay. Some years fare better than others, but in general the winemaker has set a definite style and overall quality is good. Both the Chardonnays and Cabernets may be characterized by one over-riding trait, they are well made. Either the Cabernets or Chardonnays would be wines you would be proud to serve at your table or store in your cellar.

A. Rafanelli Winery

In the Dry Creek Valley it is possible to find some of the original homesteads first settled in Sonoma County. Mary and Americo Rafanelli, owners of the A. Rafanelli Winery, live on a ranch which dates from the middle 1800s. Their vineyards and winery are situated on West Dry Creek Road in Healdsburg.

Rafanelli produces one of the only estate-bottled Zinfandels from the Dry Creek Valley (an historic area famous for the quality of this grape) which is made entirely by hand in a typically Italian style with strong grape flavors and heavy wood age. These Zinfandels are hearty, but well balanced, meant to accompany meats and pastas.

Rafanelli's love for winemaking came from his father, Albert Rafanelli, who had had a winery and vineyards in Healdsburg in the forties. His father helped him develop the hand technique of winemaking which he uses today. All his wines are made naturally with no filtering or processing.

In 1955 the Rafanellis purchased a 100 acre working ranch with a rambling farmhouse and barn with horse stables. For over a decade they harvested prunes and pears before they replanted with grapes. There are 10 acres of Gamay Beaujolais, seven acres of Zinfandel, and four acres each of Early Burgundy and French Colombard. The Zinfandels are planted on hillside vineyards in benchland soils; the other varieties are valley vineyards in gravelly loam.

"We remove the second crop of Zinfandel," says Rafanelli, an ardent believer that time should be spent in the vineyard caring for the fruit. "It gives the first crop more sugar and a better chance to develop."

Rafanelli made small amounts of wine as a hobbyist before he bonded and remodeled his redwood barn in 1974. It is designed to handle a 15,000 gallon capacity, and equipped with open redwood fermenters, wooden paddles, a basket type press (the gift of Mary's father), oak upright tanks and 100 American and French oak barrels for aging. The second level has case storage and bottling equipment.

"We do everything ourselves," says Rafanelli, pointing out how his wife Mary assists him with the chemical analyses. "I make my wines in the old European style for people who prefer a full-bodied wine."

The Rafanelli formula is not new, but it does take time. All grapes are harvested by hand in one half ton lots, then fermented from seven to ten days on the skin to obtain the most from the juice and the fruit. Rafanelli uses an old wooden paddle to turn his grapes during fermentation, so the grapes don't sit on the juice. The wine is racked (since no filtering is done) several times before put in barrel to age. Both the Zinfandel and Gamay Beaujolais (the only two wines produced) are aged for a minimum of two years in barrel before time in bottle.

Preston Vineyards

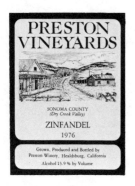

The Dry Creek district has been producing grapes for over one hundred years; it is only within the last five, however, that truly outstanding wines have appeared bearing the Dry Creek appellation. By producing wines that are well made, fairly priced, and unique in both style and character, Preston Vineyards has played a major role in this welcome development.

"We want to make a more personal statement with our wines," says Louis "Lou" Preston, winemaker and co-owner with his wife Susan. "That means growing our own grapes, making the wines ourselves and selling directly to retail stores. We will only increase production if we can maintain the individuality of our wines and the personal way of doing business."

The site of the Preston operation includes some 70 acres of vineyard running along the southern border of the Dry Creek Valley. "Here the summer days are warmer than Healdsburg because the vineyards are that much farther from the Russian River," says Preston. "The fog is not as heavy, nor does it last as long."

Over the years much has been written about the Zinfandels from these rich hillside soils. Local growers don't hesitate to boast that their Zinfandel grapes are among the finest in the county. What most of them fail to mention is the fact that, until recently, many of these same grapes met their fate in batches of mixed burgundy. Preston, however, is one winemaker who has developed a style of Zinfandel that is truly representative of the area. His Zinfandels are exciting, with berrylike aromas and peppery flavors. He chooses berries at a high degree of maturity, fermenting in open redwood and stainless steel, then aging in small oak barrels and in bottle. The winery specializes in Zinfandel and Fume Blanc, but is also currently experimenting with Cabernet Sauvignon, Merlot, Napa Gamay, and Chenin Blanc.

Preston's white wines are another indication of his talents. Made from grapes grown in benchland soils, his Fume Blancs hardly fit his modest description: "We're striving for moderately grassy wines made in the Sancerre style." By average standards, these wines are extraordinary for their individual qualities of color, aroma, body and taste as well as their characteristic regional qualities. Again the statement is in the style — Fume Blancs with the fragrance of new-mown hay and taste of ripe honeydew. Rarely has the Dry Creek Valley produced wines of such distinction.

The importance of Louis Preston's contribution goes beyond regional rivalry. Unfortunately, the future of the Dry Creek Valley is in question should the completion of the Warm Springs Dam at the western end of the valley become a reality. "We fear the consequences of the dam catalyzing uncontrolled development of the valley, with consequent downgrading of its viticultural significance," says Preston.

Field Stone Winery

FIELD STONE

ALEXANDER VALLEY
SPRING·CABERNET

Produced and Bottled by Redwood Ranch and Vineyard, Inc.
10075 State Hwy. 128, Healdsburg, CA 95448 • Alcohol 12% by Volume

Wallace Johnson of the Field Stone Winery in Healdsburg has the distinction of being one of the only vintners to develop a new process for harvesting, crushing and pressing grapes. The mobile crusher-press, a prototype of an up-and-coming commercial machine (fondly dubbed El Conejo — "the Rabbit" — by the mechanics who built it,) has the capability of setting a new quality standard for the wine industry by the quick conversion of berries into juice minutes after harvesting, with maximum retention of fragrance, flavors and freshness.

"Wine grapes are the number one agricultural product in California," says Johnson, whose firm Upright, Inc., manufactures grape harvesters and also designed the new unit. "These machines have the same significance as the cotton gin and the wheat combine."

For many years, Johnson, former mayor of Berkeley, has raised registered Hereford cattle at Redwood Ranch & Vineyards, Inc., in the Alexander Valley. In 1965, he acquired 135 acres of adjacent land which included 10 acres of Petite Sirah vineyards dating back to 1895.

This land purchase put cattle breeder Johnson into the grape growing business. In 1966, additional plantings began. Soon after, tasting wine made by Lee Stewart, original founder of Souverain Cellars,

from the Petite Sirah grapes in 1967 convinced Johnson (along with results from experimental test blocks) that Cabernet Sauvignon, Petite Sirah, Johannisberg Riesling, Gewurztraminer and Chenin Blanc grapes should be the five varieties grown at the ranch. For the past 13 years, Redwood Ranch has been selling its grapes to Souverain, Chateau Montelena, Dry Creek and Grgich Hills.

Also in 1965, the same year Redwood planted its first vineyard, Upright, Inc. started to develop a grape harvesting machine. In 1975, Chief of Research & Development Robert Fisher was given the challenging task of designing a mobile vineyard press to travel through the vineyards beside the grape harvester. His results are impressive.

Unlike other winery methods of pressing, the mobile vineyard press has the ability to convert harvested grapes into juice within two minutes. The juice is pumped continuously into a 400 gallon stainless steel tank towed behind the crusher-press. "We're harvesting juice, not grapes," says Johnson, who points out seeds and skins are then discharged onto the ground. "A vineyard can be picked at the peak of ripeness at a rate of one acre per hour. We harvest at night when it is cold (typically 55%F) rather than in the heat of the day."

The Field Stone Winery takes its name from the field stones native to Sonoma County, which form the basis of the underground facility. Here grapes are handled in as technically efficient a manner as possible using a Westphalia centrifuge, stainless steel, jacketed fermenters and American and French oak cooperage.

Alexander Valley Vineyards

Alexander Valley Vineyards lies just off Highway 128 in Healdsburg. The winery's name comes from the original owner of the property Cyrus Alexander, who was also custodian of the Rancho Sotoyome land grant for General Mariano Vallejo. The winery and vineyards lie on this historic site.

The Alexander connection dates from 1842 when Cyrus and Rufina Alexander built and occupied the first mud adobe in Sonoma County. Sales of vegetables to prospectors heading north to the California gold mines was their principal means of support.

Hank Wetzel, Jr., an executive with the Los Angeles based Garret Corporation, bought the 120 acres of property in the Alexander Valley from descendants of Alexander in 1963. Previously it had been used as pastureland for sheep and cattle. Wetzel proceeded to completely restore the Victorian mansion built by Alexander in 1848 before he moved in and made it his residence. Also on the property are two other noted Sonoma County Historical Landmarks: a remodeled 1886 Victorian Alexander Valley schoolhouse and a small wooded gravesite of the Alexander family.

Wetzel's visits to the Alexander Valley during the sixties to see Russell Green, then owner of Simi Winery, whetted Wetzel's interest in grape growing and winemaking. In 1974, a small family corporation was established. Soon after, they proceeded to develop 200 acres of vineyards featuring eight classic varieties that would do well in the gravelly loam. The Southeast end of the Alexander Valley is a mid-Region II climate with coastal intrusions that burn off by mid-morning.

"The growing climate here is cooler than the Napa Valley, especially in the fall," says winemaker Hand Wetzel, III, also a partner in the firm. "The grapes ripen more slowly. If they are too ripe, they lose a certain delicateness in the wine."

Construction of a Spanish-American two-story redwood and slumpstone winery commenced in 1973. In the fall of that year three varieties from the ranch were crushed and made into wine: Cabernet Sauvignon, Chardonnay and Johannisberg Riesling. Production the first few years was 7,000 cases. The winery was designed to house a first class operation along the lines of some of the small estates where Hank Wetzel had gotten his early training such as Freemark Abbey and Hanzell Vineyards. All the modern stainless steel equipment— fermenters and storage tanks— and French and American oak cooperage was installed.

At this moment Alexander Valley Vineyards produces 10,000 cases of premium estate-grown varietals with the Alexander Valley appellation of origin. Experimentation has taken place with Chardonnay, Johannisberg Riesling, Gewurztraminer, Chenin Blanc, Zinfandel, Pinot Noir, Merlot and Cabernet Sauvignon. All the wines are 100 percent varietals except the Cabernet Sauvignon which is blended with Merlot.

Wetzel explains their policy. "Our long term goal is not to market all the varieties we grow, but to select four or five which do the best in our area."

Johnsons' of Alexander Valley

JOHNSON'S

ALEXANDER VALLEY
1978

ALEXANDER VALLEY
CHENIN BLANC
An off dry style wine made entirely from Chenin Blanc grapes
grown in our vineyard.
OF A TOTAL OF 6,000 BOTTLES THIS IS BOTTLE NO.

Produced and bottled by
JOHNSON'S ALEXANDER VALLEY WINES
Healdsburg, Sonoma County, California
Alcohol 13.0% by Volume

Three brothers, Tom, Will and Jay Johnson are mutual proprietors and founders of the Johnson's Alexander Valley Wines located along the Russian River in Healdsburg. Their father, James Johnson, a San Francisco lawyer, purchased the ranch in 1952 with knowledge that the property had been an active winery site during the late 1800s. Upon the land are several farmhouses and a rustic barn now part of the new winery complex.

Johnson and his three sons raised pears, prunes and grapes throughout the fifties. Their fortune changed in the early sixties when low grape prices and an incurable root disease nearly wiped them out financially. By the mid-sixties new varietal vineyards and experimental winemaking turned their attention to a future in the California wine business.

In the seventies, the three brothers pooled their resources and purchased the ranch from their father. Revenue from the continued sale of prunes and pears supplemented the family-financed winery until it could pay its own way. The winery, which has some 70 acres of estate vines, was bonded in 1976 and released its first wines shortly thereafter.

Winemaker Tom Johnson explains that the family has but one goal: "We want to produce 100 percent varietals from the Johnson Ranch, using only our grapes."

Johnson's Alexander Valley Wines produces dry, estate-bottled table wines: Chardonnay, Johannisberg Riesling, Chenin Blanc, Gewurztraminer, Pinot Noir Blanc, Pinot Noir, Zinfandel and Cabernet Sauvignon. Their Rose of Pinot Noir is a delightful summer sipping wine and their dry Pear wine the only fruit wine produced in Sonoma County. The brothers will be the first Alexander Valley winery to market half bottles of a portlike Late Harvest Zinfandel, reminiscent of carmelized blackberries. Future plantings will establish their identity as the only valley producer of a dry Grenache table wine.

Jay Johnson, architect and business manager, has designed an elaborate octagonal facility, with two levels, that will house the new winery. It is made of redwood to match the other buildings on the property. The winery is constructed around a central axis with four protruding wings. It will contain the only covered production facility in the area with receivers, crushers, stemmers, presses, bottling line, case storage, offices, laboratory and tasting room. The old winery still in use houses the upright oak Yugoslavian tanks, and smaller American oak aging cellars.

Each month the Johnsons host a Sunday open house. Visitors come to taste new releases available at the winery and listen to outdoor concerts and organ recitals. The Johnsons have the distinction of owning the only two manual, seven rank, 300 pipe theatre organ, built in 1924 by Marr & Colton, in the North Coast wine country.

Says Gail Johnson, event coordinator, "We want to be known as the place in the wine country where people can come with their picnic to listen to music and enjoy our wines."

Sausal Winery

SAUSAL
1974
SONOMA COUNTY
ZINFANDEL

Produced and bottled by Sausal Winery
Alexander Valley, Ca • Alcohol 13.5% by volume

A large and twisted juniper graces the entrance to Sausal Winery in the Alexander Valley. The firm takes its name from the Sausal Creek (meaning willow in Spanish) which meanders through the property to the old quicksilver mine at Pine Flat. Geyser Peak looms in the distance.

The winery was the dream of the late Leo Demostene, once winemaker at the Soda Rock Winery in Healdsburg. Throughout the fifties, Demostene had developed the 116 acre Sausal Ranch, building a family residence on a hilltop and replacing apple and prune orchards with vineyards. In 1973, when he unexpectedly passed away, he was in the process of planning a winery. Several months later, his widow Rose Demostene, and her four children commenced construction on a redwood winery in his honor.

The winery was built at the foot of a hill from an old prune dehydrator. It was originally equipped to handle red wines with a 150,000 gallon capacity. Equipment included stainless steel jacketed fermenters, stainless storage, upright and small American oak cooperage, a bottling line and case storage.

Sausal Winery had the distinction of being a family owned and operated venture. David Demostene, who studied under his father at Soda Rock, maintains the winemaking. Edward Demostene heads the viticultural program. Rosalee Demostene acts as chemist. Lucinda Demostene Nelson manages the office. "We find that as a family concern we work best if we all work independently of each other in our areas of expertise," says Edward.

Designed primarily as a first class North Coast bulk resource, Sausal Winery sells its wines by variety to prestigious wineries in Napa, Sonoma and Mendocino counties. "A bulk facility is by far the simpler way of producing wine," says Edward; "however, you don't get quite the returns you do from bottled wine."

The Demostenes selectively cull quality grapes from three family ranches located in the Alexander and Dry Creek Valleys, which make up some 150 acres of vines.

"We are trying to make premium wines and always are looking for grapes high in sugar and high in acid," says Demostene. "If we lose some of these grapes because these factors are non-existent, we feel in the long run it's better to raise quality to get quality. Sometimes less is better."

Robert Mondavi was the gentleman who recognized this quality when he tasted some of the early batches of Sausal Zinfandel from cask. He encouraged the Demostenes to produce wine under their own label. Heeding his advice, the winery established a 1,000 case production of vintage-dated Sonoma County appellation wines and released their first wines in 1979. A White Pinot Noir was sold out months after it hit the market, and a dynamic Zinfandel, made from 70 year old vines that were dry farmed, has pleased the many mouths that have tasted it. Small bottlings of Chardonnay, Cabernet Sauvignon and a Sausal Blanc (a dry white table wine) are soon to follow.

Simi Winery

Simi Winery in Healdsburg exemplifies an old name in wine that has been affected by striking change in the American wine industry this past decade. Its founders Pietro and Giuseppe Simi would be proud of its reputation as a producer of premium North Coast varietals.

Simi began in the middle 1800's when the Simi brothers arrived in San Francisco and started a retail shop on Green Street. Grapes were transported by wagon from Sonoma to Petaluma, down the Petaluma River and across San Francisco Bay by barge and up the city's steep hills by horse cart to their winery. Success came through selling large quantities of red wines to restaurants and hotels in the Italian North Beach district and elsewhere in the California area. Expansion caused them to look to Sonoma County for a more permanent grape source and winery site.

Simi formally dates from 1876 when the brothers built a majestic stone and redwood edifice on Healdsburg Avenue. It was named Montepulciano, or "Noble Hill," for the brothers' hometown in Italy. During construction of the winery both brothers died and left Giuseppe's daughter Isabelle to run the operation.

Simi produced bulk wines before and after Prohibition and sacramental wine during Prohibition. It wasn't until Simi produced its first dry table wines and dessert wines—ports, sherries, brandies and champagne—that the winery was recognized by the public. Popularity under the commercial Montepulciano and private Hotel Del Monte (in Carmel) labels convinced Isabelle and her husband, Fred Haigh, a Healdsburg banker, to rename and promote the winery under Simi.

Russell Green, former president of Signal Oil, bought the neglected winery and its red wine inventory in 1969. He modernized the facility, outfitted it with modern stainless steel equipment and French and American oak cooperage before he restored the old stone work. Medium priced Sonoma County varietals and generics were produced.

Simi was bought and sold twice in the seventies. Scottish & Newcastle Vintners, a United States division of the Scottish whiskey and beer empire bought Simi in 1974. Two years later, Schefflin & Co., a century old New York importing firm of European lines, purchased Simi. Since then, Schefflin & Co. has continued with expansion and improvement of the winery with emphasis on new areas such as Mendocino County and old areas such as Alexander Valley from which to obtain its grapes.

Throughout both reigns of ownership Michael G. Dacres Dizon has been president and Andre Tchelistcheff, winemaker of Beaulieu Vineyards fame, has been consultant and enologist. With the advent of the eighties, Simi will make its debut into the higher priced premium wine market. Tchelistcheff explains their intentions with this move. "The Schefflin doctrine is to upgrade the quality of all its wines with far more caution and attention to the total ecological regime which includes grapes, soils and microclimates."

Souverain Cellars

Souverain Cellars stands atop a vine-laden knoll just off of Highway 101 at the Independence Lane exit in Geyserville. The John Marsh Davis-designed hop kiln winery is less than a decade old and the equipment inside just as modern, yet the story of Souverain dates from the early forties.

J. Leland Stewart, president, used the name Souverain for his first winery on Howell Mountain in the Napa Valley. Stewart popularized Souverain wines in 1949 with the first-ever bottlings of Green Hungarian, a grape used previously only for blending and subsequent bottlings of Johannisberg Riesling and Cabernet Sauvignon.

A wealthy syndicate bought Souverain, then turned around and sold it to Thomas Burgess. The investors then proceeded to build two more wineries named Souverain at sites in Rutherford in the Napa Valley and Geyserville in the Alexander Valley. During the wine boom of the seventies, the Minneapolis flour firm of The Pillsbury Company, on the recommendation of the late Princetonian Frank Schoonmaker (one of the first Americans to import French wines to the states) bought both wineries. Three years later, having lost several million, both wineries were put up for sale. Rutherford was renamed Rutherford Hill and was purchased by a group from Freemark Abbey. Alexander Valley was purchased by North Coast Cellars, a limited partnership of 240 grape growers, and renamed Souverain Cellars.

The Conegliano-educated enologist William Bonetti, thrice before winemaker at Gallo, Cresta Blanca and Charles Krug, was hired in 1972 to head the half million case premium wine program. Grapes were made available from the 240 grape growers who own the winery in Napa, Sonoma and Mendocino counties. This has offered Bonetti the opportunity to make some very exciting wines.

They include North Coast appellation oak-aged Chardonnay, Fume Blanc, Chenin Blanc, semi-dry French Colombard, Gamay and fuller-bodied Zinfandel, Pinot Noir, Petite Sirah, Cabernet Sauvignon and a dry Pinot Noir Rose. Special bottlings include a Muscat Canelli, a Cabernet Sauvignon Port and a Vintage Select Cabernet Sauvignon.

"In making wine, quality is frequently enhanced by doing less, rather than more to wine," says Bonetti.

A castle of a winery was built, with corridors for receiving and crushing, chambers for fermenting, halls for small American and French oak aging. A new cooperative storage project will add 442,000 gallons to bring total capacity, including the 300,000 oak cooperage, to a total of three million gallons.

The Restaurant at the winery, open daily, year-round for lunch and dinner, looks to the Russian River to the east and opens to a courtyard and fountain to the west. In summer, the courtyard is transformed into an open-air theatre for symphonies, musical events and dramatic plays. A guide is available on the hour to give tours and tastings.

Trentadue Winery

Evelyn and Leo Trentadue departed the Santa Clara Valley (once considered prime agricultural land) in 1959 when their orchard estate was threatened by encroaching urbanization. They moved to the Healdsburg-Geyserville area, 65 miles north of San Francisco where they founded their family owned and operated Trentadue Winery.

Trentadue, whose name means "32" in Italian, combined two of the most beautiful ranches in the upper Alexander Valley, not half a mile from the Russian River. The Luchetti Ranch had had a history of producing popular agricultural commodities. The Wisecarver Ranch, the larger of the two, had been the site of the Heart's Desire Nursery to which famed botanist Luther Burbank devoted plants and ideas.

Encouraged by past crop records, grapes being among those items grown, Trentadue planted 140 acres to vine. With the technical advice of U.C. Davis experts, Trentadue proceeded to plant one of the first *vitis vinifera* vineyards in the district. His vines, therefore, represent a spectrum of grape types, arranged in small acreage blocks. They range from noble varieties such as Chardonnay and Cabernet Sauvignon to now atypical plantings of Golden Chasselas, Early Burgundy and Carignane. All the vineyards surround the winery in the Alexander Valley, and not more than 30 percent are crushed and made into wine.

The Trentadue wines for which Leo, winemaker, and his son Victor, now his assistant, have become known are those (with some exceptions) made in the "old Italian way." The heavy white wines of the past are now being replaced with fresher and fruity white wines. These are made from oak-aged Chardonnay, Sauvignon Blanc, French Colombard, Johannisberg Riesling and Chenin Blanc. "We're seeing a move toward customers who prefer lighter white wines," says Victor, pointing to investments in temperature-controlled stainless steel fermenters.

The Trentadue reds are dry, naturally heavy dinner wines, aged for a minimum of three years in American or French oak. They are wines meant to go with food of considerable volume.

"If there's anything to say about these wines," says Victor, "it is that they are organic, with very little filtering or chemical additives."

Trentadue, also a diamond broker, has made some gems of his own. An Aleatico, a grape popular in Italy, from the dark-colored Muscat family is a spicy dessert wine most delicious when made sweet and low in alcohol. It retails for $14. A Chateau 32, a $25 California Burgundy made from the rarely occuring Botrytis cinerea, is a wine that has a "deep barky taste, a hint of sherry flavor, and both a sweet and dry finish."

Plans to expand the winery to 20,000 cases include enlarging the redwood winery, built in 1973, and adding a new crushing plant, bottling line and warehouse space. "This will allow us to increase our size as we work toward our goal of producing wine from all the grapes we grow," says Victor.

Nervo Winery

Each year generations of loyal customers from throughout California return to Nervo Vineyards on the Old Redwood Highway in Geyserville for the reasonably priced table wines for under $3.50 a bottle that have made this winery famous.

Winemaker Armand Bussone, formerly of Almaden, got the idea for his popular line of "Country Wines" from the second and third generation of Italian-American farmers who patronize Nervo and use its products as their house wine. It should be pointed out that the winery was established in 1908 as a local producer of heavy, well aged, wood-style table wines.

The Nervo Country Wines include a Red, White and Vin Rose, all acceptable and fairly priced; a sweet, but refreshing when cold Winterchill, a vin ordinaire dubbed Farmer's Red, and a bargain-priced Cabernet Sauvignon.

"Our customers are our old friends," says Carreras, "and come to enjoy the peaceful setting, the arbored picnic area and the casual atmosphere."

What guests and visitors come to see is not a working winery (as Nervo is primarily designed as a sales outlet and oak aging center), but to catch a glimpse of Sonoma's wine past. The story dates from 1896 when Frank Nervo, Sr., and his bride Maria arrived in the Sonoma Valley from Venice. They were drawn west by tales of wine flowing like water from the California Valleys. Nervo bought 250 acres on two sides of the Old Redwood Highway, 10 acres of which was cultivated vineyard. From the highway east to the Russian River, was a tangle of oak trees and brush, which Nervo cleared, plowed and planted to grapes, primarily Zinfandel, with some Alicante, Golden Chasselas, Malvasia and Carignane.

In 1908 the present winery was constructed from stone quarried above the Alexander Valley. Timbers for the roof were shipped to the site from Oregon by rail. Redwood aging tanks were installed on the upper level and a small crusher-stemmer placed below. The must was piped upstairs by steam power, and after fermentation, lowered by hand to the press. The finished wine was shipped in barrel to New Orleans, Chicago, New York and San Francisco.

Through Prohibition the wine remained in redwood tanks. Upon Repeal of Prohibition, the Nervos enlarged the winery and opened a retail sales room. Sales, at first, were Burgundy, Claret, Zinfandel and Sauterne by the 50-gallon barrel. In 1905, the old vineyards were replaced with Pinot Noir, Pinot St. Georges, Beclan and Cabernet Sauvignon. As grapes came of age, the winery became a favorite stopping place for those who liked heavy red wines.

Nervo Winery has been purchased by the Joseph Schlitz Brewing Co., also owners of neighboring Geyser Peak Winery.

J. Pedroncelli Winery

It was to the Canyon Road foothills in the flat of the fog-shrouded Russian River watershed that John Pedroncelli came in 1927 to found the J. Pedroncelli Winery in Geyserville.

Pedroncelli Winery made Sonoma table wines, primarily Claret, Burgundy and Chablis, and the rest bulk wines from hillside vineyards near the 1904 J. Canata Winery he purchased from the wholesale grocer and proprietor of that name. Fifty gallon barrels and one-gallon jugs, popular sizes amongst his Italian restaurant and retail patrons, were the volume items of the day. In the forties, and again in the fifties, demands for new grape types, specifically Zinfandel and Pinot Noir, caused Pedroncelli to expand his selection.

Since 1963, Pedroncelli's two sons, John, an ardent hunter, and Jim, an outdoorsman, who were both born, raised and bred Sonoma farm boys knowing wine, assumed formal ownership of the winery from their father. The aging senior Pedroncelli, by then well into his seventies, wished to lighten his responsibilities and retired.

Brothers John, who had made wine under the tutelage of his father from 1952, and Jim made plans to increase case production to 60,000. Production emphasis was placed on the classical varieties with fermentation in stainless steel tanks and aging in stainless steel and oak.

The 135 acres of vineyard, all located in the Dry Creek Valley watershed, supply one-third of the grape requirements, with the balance coming from independent growers in the Dry Creek and Alexander Valleys near the winery. The estate vines are planted to Cabernet Sauvignon, 25 acres; Chardonnay, eight acres; Johannisberg Riesling, 12 acres; Pinot Noir, 18 acres; Gewurztraminer, 10 acres; Gamay, 10 acres; Zinfandel, 30 acres; French Colombard, six acres; and Carignane, six acres. "These rolling benchland soils produce more flavor and color in the skins," says Jim.

The premises have been enlarged some eight times to present capacity of 560,000 gallons and annual case production of over 100,000. Among the wines produced here, all have a vintage date and Sonoma County appellation, with equal emphasis on reds and whites.

We try to maintain a medium-price range," says Jim. "It is our market strategy to price for quality. People talk about $10 and $20 bottle prices, but most consumers don't buy in that area. A knowledgeable winemaker can make sales producing good wine at fair prices."

Year after year, Pedroncelli wines get better and better. Varietal flavors are improving as more attention and technique are applied to specific grape types.

"We're looking for big volume in our day to day bulk wines," says Jim, "but our better wines are becoming more flavorful, some dry, but not completely dry with softer, fuller touches."

Geyser Peak Winery

The 3600 foot prominence of Geyser Peak names both the winery and the summit it faces. It was, in fact, the nearby geysers and mineral springs that lured German visitor Augustus Quitzow who constructed a handsome winery, north of Geyserville, in 1880. He soon added a sturdy distillery.

Quitzow sold in 1887 to New York importers and wholesaler of quality brandies, Edward Walden. After the turn of the century, the winery changed hands several times again until 1937, when it was acquired by the Bagnani family, who retained the winery for 35 years.

Giuseppe Bagnani made bulk wines at the Geyserville winery and his sons controlled the country's first vineyard company on Montgomery Street in San Francisco. Known for their Four Monk's label, the Bagnani family had been making wine vinegar since 1932 and continues to hold the Federal Alcohol Tax License No. 1.

When Giuseppe died in 1952, his son Dante took over the winery. He continued bulk wine production and says that he posted the following sign at the winery to discourage visitors: Sorry, no retail sales. We drink it all.

The sleepy little winery began a rapid transformation in 1972 when the Bagnanis voted to sell the operation to the Joseph Schlitz Brewing Company. Dante Bagnani was asked to stay on as vice president of operations.

The old redwood barn, circa 1880, was preserved to set the architectural style of the new winery buildings. Santa Rosa architect, Richard Keith, designed a facility from redwood and fieldstone that blended with the natural slope of the hill. The modern stainless steel fermentation center stands side by side with the 100-year-old redwood tanks and smaller imported wooden cooperage. The grounds are elegantly landscaped with stone terraces, flowing fountain and wrought iron gates. Across the Old Redwood Highway, a 50,000 square foot storage area will be constructed with new bottling line, laboratory and storage facility.

The year 1980 marked the 100th anniversary of Geyser Peak. In celebration of their history, Armand Bussone, winemaster, and George Vare, president, have dedicated all case production (with significant volume increases in the future) to "high quality premium wines available to the public at reasonable prices."

Northcoast labels will be featured for both lines. The Geyser Peak, vintage-dated premium line of table wines will ultimately feature many estate wines made from the 625 acres of vines under cultivation, and not yet fully bearing, within the vineyard complex of the winery. Now growers throughout California supply the main grape source.

The Summit label, a non-vintaged, medium-priced line of table wines is made up of Chablis, Winterchill, Rhine, Zinfandel and Vin Rose.

Pastori Winery

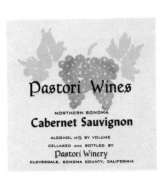

Pastori Wines

NORTHERN SONOMA

Cabernet Sauvignon

ALCOHOL 13% BY VOLUME

CELLARED AND BOTTLED BY

Pastori Winery

CLOVERDALE, SONOMA COUNTY, CALIFORNIA

The Pastori name has been associated with wines in northern Sonoma County since 1914 when the dashing Constante Pastori and his attractive young wife, Ermina, emigrated from their home in Italy to Geyserville.

An 110 acre ranch, located in the heart of the valley along the edge of the Russian River, became their home. Having acquired an appreciation of wine from his Italian forefathers, the young Constante attempted to simulate his European experience the best he could and planted vineyards and built a redwood winery nearby. Some 60 acres were planted to vines, primarily of Zinfandel, Petite Sirah and Carignane.

Processing followed Italian traditions with emphasis on hand labor, picking in the cool of the morning, fermenting in open redwood, racking again and again, and aging for several years in wood to produce heavy wines of vin ordinaire quality. For the most part wines were made and sold in bulk by variety and the remainder went to neighbor Italian Swiss Colony.

Prohibition all but closed the winery down, but wine rested safely in cask during this period. From the Repeal of Prohibition until 1947, the winery produced in bulk capacity, bottling some varieties in fifths, and selling the rest. Constante's death, also in 1947, caused sudden change in the direction and ownership of the firm. In 1948, the winery was put up for sale and became absorbed into another winery operation also in Sonoma County.

Frank Pastori, only son of the founder, had apprenticed under his father to learn to make wine. It was always his intention to some day build a winery of his own. From 1948, Frank and his wife Edith Pastori leased a 200 acre ranch upon which they cultivated wine grapes for commercial usage. These grapes included Zinfandel, Cabernet Sauvignon, Pinot Noir, Pinot St. George, Johannisberg Riesling and Chenin Blanc. Frank Nervo, Sr., of the Nervo Vineyards, which is located just to the south of the Pastori Ranch, bought these grapes from the Pastoris from which to make his Nervo table wines. From 1964 to 1973, Pastori worked with Nervo making wine at the Nervo Winery.

It was only in 1975, in the middle of the wine boom, that Frank Pastori started his own winery and put the family name back into business. On the site of an old prune hydrator he constructed a 50,000 gallon capacity winery. It was equipped with a mixture of brand new stainless steel jacketed fermenters, stainless storage, old redwood upright tanks and small American and French oak cooperage. Pastori's first wines under his own label were purchased wines (that he finished) that had once been part of the Nervo Vineyards inventory.

Today Pastori produces North Coast appellation wines, all vintage-dated and estate-bottled not exceeding 5,000 cases a year. These wines are characteristically heavier red table wines, with lots of wood, from Cabernet Sauvignon, Pinot Noir, Pinot St. George, Zinfandel, Chenin Blanc, Johannisberg Riesling and Burgundy.

Giuseppi Mazzoni

Giuseppi Mazzoni, a young adventurer, left his home near the marble ruins of Carrara, Italy, at the turn-of-the-century, voyaged by clipper ship to New York, then by train to San Francisco. Working in the gardens of Colma, south of the bay city, provided Mazzoni with enough capital to finance a ranch in Cloverdale 70 miles north of San Francisco.

The rolling countryside, which had a strong resemblance to the vineyardland near his homeland, was smothered in spreading oak and twisted madrone. The land was cleared and planted to Zinfandel and Carignane. It should be noted that Mazzoni is cited in numerous texts as one of the pioneer vineyardists in northern Sonoma County experimenting with Zinfandel. Some of these early vines, still bearing, produce crops of high sugars, good acids, low yields and of substance to make an exciting wine.

By 1912 the Mazzoni Ranch was divided into two farms. The upper ranch was developed into a winery and vineyard for Mazzoni's next of kin. The lower ranch, along Chianti Road, is the site of the present winery and vineyard.

Construction commenced on the 80,000 gallon redwood winery in 1915. It was equipped entirely with redwood, from open fermenters to upright tanks. Most of the bulk wine produced was sold to Italian Swiss Colony and the Petri Wine Co.

Giuseppi Mazzoni made wine, assisted by his two sons, James and Frederick, in the Italian traditions. Fermentations were slow and natural, wines were racked consistently, then aged in redwood up to three years to produce heavy style wines.

The Mazzoni Winery was active until the Dry years, then ceased production in 1938. Fred Mazzoni revived the family firm that year, bottling in gallons for customers who bought wine at retail from the winery or at the family wine shop on Powell Street in San Francisco.

Today very little has changed at the winery. Fred Mazzoni, now advancing in years, has limited production to what he can handle, around 2,000 cases annually. Mazzoni harvests 40 acres, including Carignane, Zinfandel, Golden Chasselas, Burger and French Colombard. The rest is sold to local vintners for special bottlings. Mazzoni produced two non-vintaged California table wines: a Burgundy and a Chablis. The dry Chablis, a slightly heavier white wine than is typical of the popular style of the day, is a blend of Golden Chasselas, Burger and French Colombard. The Burgundy, by far the better of the two, is an excellent blend of Carignane and Zinfandel, and one of the best buys for a house wine in the area.

Mazzoni wines are rarely advertised, and are only available at the winery by the $10 case lot throughout the business week and on Sundays when Mazzoni may be found at home. These are historic wines, ones to taste and not to be missed for the mere perspective they place on the importance of "wines made heavy with lots of wood that are neither finished or pasteurized."

Vina Vista Vineyards

Vina Vista

Sonoma
1973 ZINFANDEL

PRODUCED AND BOTTLED BY VINA VISTA WINERY
GEYSERVILLE, CALIFORNIA
ALCOHOL 12.9% BY VOLUME

Northern County Zinfandels, rich and well-aged like raspberries, made from 60-year-old stressed vines, are the specialty of Vina Vista Vineyards in Geyserville.

The 113 acre country property, poised on a ridge overlooking the upper Russian River region and east to Geyser Peak, was so named by its present owners in testimony of the panoramic view of vineyardland surrounding the winery.

Since 1970, Kansas-born schoolteacher Elizabeth Nelson and her space communications engineer husband Keith, with financial support from a small group of investors, have owned and managed the winery that previously belonged to descendants of the Giuseppi Mazzoni family. It was not without consideration that the Nelsons took on the task of commuting weekends from their home in Santa Clara County to Sonoma County to start yet a second fulltime business. "Although the winery hasn't always been profitable," muses Nelson, "in time it will eventually pay for itself."

Vina Vista owns no vineyards (although studies are currently being made to evaluate upper elevation soils for vines), but buys from local North Coast vineyardists. "The Zinfandels are among the best in the area with high sugars and natural acids," says Nelson.

Sonoma County appellation wines, Zinfandel, Petite Sirah, Cabernet Sauvignon, Chardonnay and Johannisberg Riesling, are the main dinner wines emphasized. All these wines are 100 percent varietal, handled individually in 1000 gallon lots.

The technique used to make these wines requires attention to temperature-controlled stainless steel fermentations and a combination of aging in stainless steel and oak. Chardonnays, fermented to extreme dryness, and Johannisberg Rieslings, fermented to medium dryness that are light and fruity are the style of the white wines offered. The Cabernet Sauvignon, Zinfandels, and Petite Sirahs are full and round and age no less than three years in American oak barrels.

"I want to work with the best extreme varietal wines and do the absolute minimal amount of processing," says Nelson.

He makes his point further, using a four year old Zinfandel as an example, a wine that lives on long after bottling. Nelson explains that all these grapes are hand-picked, then slowly and naturally fermented to dryness on the skins, racked before allowed to settle in oak. "The wines are totally unfiltered and unclarified throughout their development," he says. "I let the wine make itself. I merely rack it again and again."

Vina Vista Vineyards plans gradual expansion to accommodate 5,000 cases by the mid-eighties. An enclosed fermentation site, new bottling line and case storage will be constructed in front of the present redwood winery building constructed in 1973. The Nelsons will move to their new mountain-top residence, as plans progress, and fulfill their life's dream to make the rural wine industry their business and lifestyle.

Italian Swiss Colony

Italian Swiss Colony at Asti is one of the largest, historic, famous wineries in the world. To millions of people, from coast to coast and continent to continent, Italian Swiss Colony means good wines at affordable prices.

The story of Asti dates from 1881 when Andrea Sbarboro, a man of many initiatives, formed a cooperative agricultural association for jobless Swiss and Italian immigrants recently arrived in California.

Called the Italian Swiss Agricultural Colony, it was made up of prominent members of the Italian community. They included Mark J. Fontana (chairman of the largest canning company in the world) as president; Dr. Giuseppe Ollino as vice president; Henry Cassanova as treasurer; and Dr. Paola De Vecchi and Andrea Sbarboro as secretaries.

The Colony was designed to provide board, room and wages on condition that each worker would promise to buy five shares per month in the Colony at a dollar per share, thus building equity in their own vineyard. The cooperative approach was turned down by the workers, and Sbarboro established a private enterprise.

It was one of the ambitions of the founders to duplicate, if possible, the wines familiar to the Italians (and Swiss) who had left their homeland. The land selected for this venture was the rolling hillsides of upper Sonoma at Asti, with soil and temperature conditions closely resembling Central Italy. Twenty-five hundred acres were purchased at a price of $25,000.

In the late 1880's Dr. G. Ollino, vice president, then in Italy was entrusted with obtaining cuttings from vineyards of Europe, particularly those of Italy. Among the Italian varieties selected and sent to California were Barbera, Grignolino and some of the varieties of Chianti among which was primarily Sangioveto (also pronounced Sangiovese).

In 1887 the first winery building of brick and stone was built at Asti. The first harvest, however, was a disaster, and the wine turned to vinegar. This pattern repeated itself until the enologist from the University of Turin Pietro Rossi started to make dry table wines that won medals and awards throughout the United States and Europe.

Selling wine for profit was more difficult. When seven cents a gallon was all the Colony could get for their wine, they became their own agents, wholesaling to retailers for 30 to 50 cents a gallon in New Orleans, Chicago and New York.

By then, the expanded Colony holdings represented some 5,000 acres of vines, not to mention an equal quantity that was purchased each year, and eight wineries, some of the largest in California. Their properties included Asti, Fulton and Sebastopol in Sonoma County, at Madera in Madera County, at Lemoore in King County and at Selma in Fresno County, with storage vaults in San Francisco and New York. At Asti, an excavation was made for a cement cistern for aging wines up to 500,000 gallons.

Tipo Chianti, a red and white table wine, dressed in a straw covered Italian fiaschi became the popular

El Carmelo Chapel at Asti

wine of the day. For about one decade, the wine was known as "Tipo Chianti," but in 1906, the Colony registered the name "Tipo" eliminating the word "Chianti" and thereafter called their wines "Tipo Red" and "Tipo White."

The Asti community, with its olive trees, orange groves and vineyard estates and magnificent villas, constructed by the founders, was visited by royalty and dignitaries world-wide. All of them were awed by this self-contained community with its El Carmelo Chapel, (in the shape of a wine cask), its schools, shops, homes, parks and gardens.

The year 1911 brought French Champagnemaster Charles Jadeau to Asti to make the first sparkling wines at the Colony. The Grand Prix, the highest award given at the Exposition in Turin, Italy, as many others before, was presented to the directors for their Extra Golden Dry Champagne.

That same year, tragedy came to Asti when Pietro Rossi was thrown from a horse and killed. Two years later, the California Wine Association, a powerful conglomerate of wineries throughout California that controlled the supply of wine up until Prohibition bought the Colony. More misfortune followed. Sbarboro, who had remained as secretary, had fought the Prohibitionists from the beginning — delivering ardent speeches, writing pamphlets and appearing before congressional committees. He espoused table wine consumption as the alternative to the hard liquor habit. Continually opposed, he finally realized that his effort was but a delaying action, and soon after resigned from the wine business entirely.

From 1920, twins Edmund and Robert Rossi, with their colleague Enrico Prati, bought back the Colony from the California Wine Association, producing table grapes, concentrate and grape juice. With the Repeal of Prohibition, the owners once again worked to build the Colony line.

Just prior to World War II, then enjoying its fame as one of the top three wineries in America, whiskey firm National Distillers assumed ownership. By 1953, United Vintners were major stockholders.

Since the Heublein-United Vintners Association, the Colony has concentrated on a line of non-vintaged wines. In the white selections, Chablis and Rhineskeller Moselle are amongst the best sellers; in the red collection Colony Chianti, always a favorite along with the Tipo Chianti, and the Cabernet Sauvignon and Burgundy. Also of interest are the "pop" flavored wines, made at Madera, California such as Bali Hai, Sangrole and the T.J. Swann line with names like Mellow Days, Easy Nights and Stepping Out. The Classic Dry Sherry has gained in popularity as an aperitif, the Straight Velvet Cream Sherry and Fireside Port as after dinner or evening wines.

Jade Mountain

JADE MOUNTAIN
Sonoma County
CABERNET SAUVIGNON
1975

Jade Mountain was founded in 1975 by Dr. Douglass Cartwright, a Jungian analyst, and his wife, Lillian Cartwright, a psychologist. Their charming wood and stone country house and their weathered wooden winery are located on their ranch in the rugged terrain southwest of Cloverdale.

The ranchland is made up of a series of hills and valleys, accented with canyons, glens and waterways. Doctor Cartwright named the dominant elevation which rises out of a chain of deeply wooded green mountains, Jade Mountain. The name Jade Mountain is the title of a Chinese anthology containing a collection of 300 poems from the T'ang Dynasty.

On the hillsides around the ranch are the remains of gnarled vineyards which Dr. Cartwright believes were planted by the early settlers in the late 1880's. In the late afternoon when the sun hits the hillsides at a certain angle, lines left from the furrowed vineyards may be seen. In the early 1900's the Newman family acquired the property which contained the remains of a working winery.

When Dr. Cartwright purchased the property in 1959, there were several old buildings badly in need of repair. In the barn, he found old pumps, wooden cooperage and wine artifacts which were used by the previous winemakers. In the early seventies, Dr. Cartwright renovated the old barn into a serviceable winery.

Surrounding the winery are 31 acres of vineyard located on the valley floor and hillsides. The additional pastureland is used to graze sheep and cattle while deer, quail and wild pig roam the back country. There are 19 acres of Cabernet Sauvignon; 7 acres of Riesling and five acres of hillside which have not been budded. Until 1974, the Cartwrights sold their grapes to other wineries. However, their enjoyment of fine wines led them to take a more serious approach to the art of winemaking.

The entire Cartwright family shares an interest in wines and rustic living. On weekends, it is not unusual to find the Cartwrights and their four children David, Derrick, Katy and Rosanna helping in the vineyard or winery. The children have found Pomo Indian arrowheads and pottery which were uncovered by tractors. A tall, lone pine dominates the hill above the vineyards. According to young Derrick Cartwright, an enthusiastic naturalist, it most likely is the burial site of a Pomo Indian chief.

As a 2,000 gallon producer, Jade Mountain will make only two vintage-dated, estate bottled selections, a German-style Riesling and a distinctive California Cabernet Sauvignon. Clarets are aged in 60 gallon French and Never oak casks.

"Our intent is to preserve a certain quality of family life in a positive, cooperative farming venture at Jade Mountain. Life is less in the being and more in the becoming," concludes Dr. Douglass Cartwright.

Jade Mountain is an honest effort to create fine wine on a modest scale and budget with the enthusastic participation of family.

A. Rege Wine Co.

A fleet of English delivery vans sit atop the hillside vineyard to the west of Highway 101 just before the Dutcher Creek exit in Cloverdale. Big block letters, which can be seen by travelers going either direction, read the "A. Rege Wine Co."

These vans, long since replaced with flatbed trucks, are reminders of an era gone by in the wine business when the vintner who made the wine personally delivered it to the customer. Such is the intriguing story of this second generation American wine company founded by Alfonso Rege in 1932.

A San Francisco sheet metal worker-turned-wine-grower, Alfonso bought a 52 acre spread in the northern Sonoma farm country. He built a house, constructed a barn and planted a vineyard, all above the Russian River.

Rege was a homewinemaker who concocted experimental blends for family and friends. Giving their approval, they encouraged Alfonso to make his avocation his vocation. In 1937, construction commenced on a rectangular redwood 150,000 gallon winery. It was designed to produce bulk wines, and equipped modestly with open concrete fermenters and redwood holding tanks.

By 1939, Alfonso was making wine and selling it commercially from the winery. As business increased, he enlarged his marketing capacity and in 1940 opened a quaint Old World retail wine shop in San Francisco's Italian North Beach district on Powell Street. Alfonso's grand-nephew, David Rege, now owns and operates the shop and sells Rege wines amongst others.

Alfonso Rege died in 1947 and his two sons, Hector and Eugene, who had grown up on the farm became joint owners. They continued to maintain the winery in much the same style of winemaking as their father, creating gutsy wines to go with heavy foods.

In 1969, shortly after the death of Hector Rege, Eugene and his wife Adamae Rege became sole proprietors. They purchased a neighboring ranch and increased their acreage to 94. Today there are 84 acres of vines under cultivation which supply grapes for wine. They include Cabernet Sauvignon, Petite Sirah, Pinot Noir, Carignane, Zinfandel, Napa Gamay, Golden Chasselas and Burger. These grapes make up the California-designated, non-vintaged line of generics. In order of popularity they feature a dry but heavy Rege Reserve Chablis, made from a mixture of Golden Chasselas and Burger, a Chateau Rege Burgundy, a blend of Carignane, Petite Sirah and Zinfandel, and an Alfonso Rege Vin Rose. All the wines retail for $3.50 a gallon or less. The premium Rege vintage-dated varietals, made from purchased California wines at $3.00 a fifth and under, list a Cabernet Sauvignon, Pinot Noir, Barbera, Gamay Beaujolais, Chenin Blanc, and Green Hungarian.

The retail sales room, open daily from nine to five except Sundays, attracts customers from families around the area. "People seem to know we're here," says Adamae Rege, "so we just keep on making the wine, trying to keep our customers happy."

Bandiera Wines

BANDIERA

Sonoma County
ZINFANDEL

Made and Bottled by Bandiera Winery·Cloverdale, California
Alcohol 13% by Volume·Bonded Winery 3998

When telling the great coastal redwoods in Mendocino County no longer proved sufficient income for Emil Bandiera, lumberman, and his supportive wife, Ludina, they moved to the farming country of Cloverdale in northern Sonoma County.

Prior to Prohibition, Cloverdale had supported over a dozen active wineries, but during the Repeal years, this small town practically ignored its winemaking heritage and turned its attention to citrus cultivation. From 1927, when the Bandieras purchased their 78 acre Cherry Creek Road Ranch in the western foothills of the town, they had had dreams of reviving this winemaking tradition and founding a winery. Oak and madrone-covered hillsides were cleared and planted to Zinfandel, Carignane, Grenoir and Golden Chasselas. Ripened fruit, once harvested, was shipped by rail to Petaluma, then taken by boat to the market on the San Francisco waterfront.

Bandiera Wines date from 1937 when the first hand-tended wines, made in the 1935 manzanita-covered redwood winery, were released to the public. The wines were bottled and sold in fifths, by the 50-gallon barrels or in demi-johns and half gallons customers brought with them.

Emil Bandiera died in 1964 and left his son Ralo, who had apprenticed under him in winemaking, to manage the winery. Ralo maintained a working winery until the early seventies, then streamlined the opera-

tion by introducing purchased wines he finished and bottled. Thus sales under the Bandiera name continued as usual at the winery, but the winemaking activities ceased.

Chris Bilbro, grandson of the founder, and Marc Black, a close Cloverdale friend, formed a partnership in 1975 and bought the Bandiera Winery. Both men had worked at the winery previously and pledged to become premium producers solely of red North Coast varieties. All of their vintage-dated table wines from their premium line are made from either purchased grapes or wines from the Alexander Valley. They include Cabernet Sauvignon, Petite Sirah, Pinot Noir, Zinfandel and Gamay.

Special attention, when possible, has been spent finding older Sonoma vineyards from which to make individual lots of regional wines. One of Bilbro's favorite wines is a Zinfandel from the 50-year-old vines owned by neighbor Giuseppe Mazzoni. This wine was fermented naturally, long on the skins with aging in small French and American oak.

"We make very sturdy, full-bodied wines," explains Bilbro, winemaker, also pointing out the importance of the sophisticated medium price wine audience they are after, "around 13 percent alcohol with high sugars that are balanced by good acids."

The secondary label Bandiera carafe wines, from California sources, are available in metric sizes. The popularly priced Zinfandel is a blended wine, 85 percent from northern Sonoma grapes, the remainder from Lodi grapes. The Burgundy, also a blend, is part Zinfandel and part Carignane with a slightly higher residual sugar.

Jordan Vineyard and Winery, located in the hills of the Alexander Valley, gives eloquent testimony to the commitment of its owners, Tom and Sally Jordan. Beginning in 1972 with the purchase of vineyard land at the base of the winery's hilltop site, the Jordans have painstakingly developed a completely integrated vineyard and winery operation, patterned in the classical chateau tradition.

Through the course of the systematic development of vineyard and winery, Jordan has attracted nearly a score of talented craftsmen and technicians. The carefully maintained vineyards and the purposeful order seen in the winery give ample evidence of their expertise, as well as their sense of mutual pride. The responsibility for the development and direction of both vineyard and winery rests with Mike Rowan, who has worked with the Jordans from the beginning of their undertaking.

The winery building reflects the influence of French provincial architecture. This beautiful structure is distinguished by the harmony of its design and the caliber of the craftsmanship employed in its construction.

Incorporated within is a winemaking operation that is distinctly Californian in its blend of tradition and technology. Beauty and function are skillfully combined with neither being slave to the other.

Frank Woods, chairman of the board of the corporation that controls Clos du Bois in Healdsburg, has come up with an imaginative formula for marketing wine, which keeps quality high and prices down.

Winemaker Thomas Hobart has the challenging opportunity to produce vintage-dated, estate-bottled wines from 100 percent varietals from a first class appellation. What is more they are equal in quality and price to other top competitors in the 20,000 case range.

Clos du Bois produces five estate wines under their premium label from 300 acres of corporate owned vineyards in the Dry Creek and Alexander Valleys. The Chardonnay, Gewurztraminer and Johannisberg Riesling all come from the latter mentioned valley. Among these wines the Gewurztraminers are extremely well made. "The ocean influence, clay soils and good drainage are excellent here," says Woods.

The Cabernet Sauvignons, and Pinot Noirs originate from the Dry Creek Valley. Made big with lots of flavor and tannin, these wines are aged in small French oak cooperage. The Pinot Noirs from these vineyards are exceptional. "The Dry Creek Valley produces high sugars and excellent tannins," he concludes.

Robert Stemmler of the Dry Creek Valley is no newcomer to the wine business, but wines appearing under his proprietary label are a more recent development.

Since 1970, with studies in enology at Bad Kreuznach and 10 years previous experience at Charles Krug and Inglenook, he has lived in Sonoma County. In 1974 Trumbull W. Kelly of Sacramento joined him in partnership to found a winery.

"I always wanted to make wine in my style," says Stemmler, "one which would attract a small following."

The small, but modern winery on Lambert Bridge Road is surrounded by four acres of Pinot Chardonnay from Napa Valley clones. The Cabernet Sauvignon is supplied by local North Coast growers. Stemmler's enjoyment comes from working with these two wines in closely monitored lots. "I like to bring out the best in each batch," he says.

Presently availability will not exceed 2,000 cases annually. The wines, all thought-provoking, are priced from eight dollars a bottle and represent yet another dimension of winemaking from the Dry Creek Valley.

"I want to make dry table wines as naturally as possible," says Stemmler. "These wines are meant to be enjoyed... to be consumed, not sipped."

The name "Lytton Springs" conjures up images of rich, lush full-bodied Zinfandels reminiscent of raspberries from very old vines. The Lytton Springs Winery located on Lytton Springs Road exit off of Highway 101 in Healdsburg specializes in fine wines from this one varietal.

The almost 50 acres of very old established vines, called the Valley Vista Vineyards, are owned by a consortium headed by *Wine World Magazine* editor Dee Sindt and managers Grace and Bura Walters. Since 1970, these vines have supplied wineries like Ridge Vineyards of Cupertino with grapes to produce some of the most talked-about Zinfandels in the state.

In 1977 winemaker Walters produced 5,000 cases of estate Zinfandel under the Lytton Springs Winery label in the traditional Sonoma Cellars. Says Walters, "We believe in making Zinfandel from old vineyards with low yield of high quality grapes."

The Lytton Springs Zinfandels, available for $6.50 and up, are all vintage dated and oak aged. "Typically our Zinfandels are heavy, unfiltered wines with the minimal amounts of chemicals used in processing," explains Walters.

California

Mendocino
Wineries

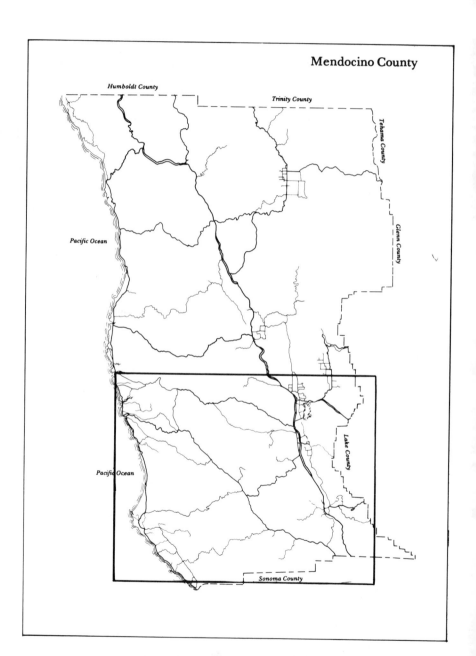

Mendocino County

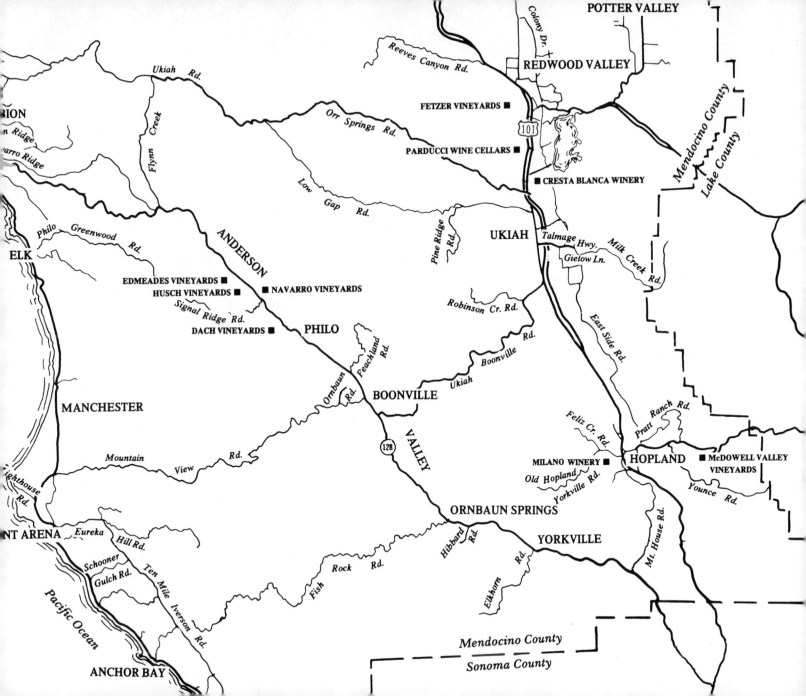

Navarro Vineyards

One of the more positive trends of the seventies has been the way in which the wine business has attracted talented professionals away from other fields and inspired them to start wineries of their own. Such was the case with Deborah Cahn, a U.C. Berkeley English major, and her husband Edward Bennett, former vice president of a chain of high fidelity stores, who in 1974 founded Navarro Vineyards in Mendocino county.

"We always loved wine," explains Cahn. "We looked to the cooler Anderson Valley to develop German style Gewurztraminers and White Rieslings and French Chardonnays and Pinot Noirs."

Raising sheep for wool and growing grapes for wine; the combination so appealed to Cahn and Bennett that they bought 910 acres of heavily wooded Mendocino backcountry near the Coastal Range. "The coastal influence is so predominant here," remarks Cahn, "that it's cooler at one in the afternoon than eleven o'clock in the morning."

With imagination and innovation, the owners cleverly adapted what used to be the John Williams sheep ranch into a rustic, country wine operation. A weathered hay barn was remodeled into an attractive living quarters; a new sheep barn was built in the style of the traditional Mendocino sheep barn and used for the winery; and vineyards were ingeniously designed to follow the lay of the land.

"We were one of the first wineries in Mendocino county to develop hillside vineyards on the contour," explains Cahn, who ran into difficulties when trying to find a similar experimental vineyard in the county. Nevertheless by 1975, Cahn and Bennett felt assured that the concept was viable and simultaneously planted their first vineyards: 30 acres of Gewurztraminer; 5 acres of Pinot Noir; and 10 acres of Chardonnay. They also released the first Mendocino county Gewurztraminer under the Navarro Vineyards label from purchased Anderson Valley grapes.

"We're continually working to capture the Gewurztraminer spice and flavor," comments Bennett. He uses this grape as one example of his research to pinpoint the best growing areas. "The vineyards in this area produce good fruit and acids hold up well."

Navarro Vineyards is made up of a dynamic team of personalities with special expertise. Bennett oversees the long-term direction of the winery and makes wine; Texas Sawyer, who has his master's from U.C. Davis, is the technician and assistant winemaker; Dan Baron, also a graduate of U.C. Davis, heads up the viticultural department; and Deborah Cahn sells and markets the wine.

Navarro Vineyards has shown great interest in helping to pioneer a newly emerging wine district — the Anderson Valley. The spirit of their new enterprise is characterized by Deborah Cahn when she says, "When you can trade three lambs and six cases of wine for delivery of a baby, you have a nice feeling that your life and work are intimately self-sufficient."

Husch Vineyards

Tony and Gretchen Husch had not ordered their lives in preparation for the profession of winegrower. Their common meeting ground, in fact, had been graduate work in city planning at the University of Berkeley. Tony, a native of St. Louis, Missouri, had done his undergraduate work at Harvard University in Massachusetts. Gretchen, who grew up in Maryland, had studied at Sarah Lawrence College in New York, then later became an artist.

The couple resolved to quit the city for the simpler country life when Tony expressed a strong desire "to plant grapes and make wine." So, in time, the Husches bought 60 acres of the old Nunn Ranch in Mendocino County, which had been a successful grain and apple operation.

In the late sixties, they planted their first vineyards—some eight acres of terraced land with southwestern exposure on the slopes above the Navarro River. By the early seventies, they had some 25 acres of Chardonnay and Gewurztraminer and Pinot Noir in full production. By the late seventies, they also decided to purchase Johannisberg Riesling and Cabernet Sauvignon from neighboring Mendocino growers. It should be noted that all these grapes are admirably suited to the cool Anderson Valley clime. The Pacific Ocean is but 12 miles to the west, and early morning fogs often keep thermometer readings noticeably lower than in the Ukiah or Redwood areas. Because the grapes mature more slowly and retain so much of their acidity, the wines from the area take on a good deal of their natural varietal character.

In 1971, winemaking began in temporary facilities. Grapes, hand-picked into 40 pound lug boxes, were crushed on the small patio in back of the Husch home. As the couple gained experience, their operation slowly grew. In 1973, chemist Al White joined Tony. The following year, a new and well-equipped winery, whose exterior was designed to look like barns common to the area, was built. Today, its 15,000 gallon capacity will handle the full production of all produced and purchased grapes. "We've attained our goal in terms of size," explains Gretchen.

The Husch Winery is located at the western end of the Anderson Valley, about midway between Philo and Navarro on California State Highway 128. Next to the winery is the sales room, carefully remodeled from an old granary. In addition to the Husch wines, Gretchen's watercolors of vineyards, other landscapes and seascapes are also on display and for sale. The sales room is open daily from ten until five, and visitors are invited to make use of the shady picnic area close by.

The Husch label, which Gretchen designed, shows a young couple silhouetted in a row of vines. It is an expression of the idealism and enthusiasm brought to their vocation by Gretchen and Tony Husch.

Edmeades Vineyards

EDMEADES VINEYARDS

ANDERSON VALLEY HEALTH CENTER
California
CABERNET SAUVIGNON

Alcohol 13.1% by volume
Cellared & Bottled by Edmeades Vineyards
Philo, Mendocino County, California

To aid in supporting the one source of health care in our remote,
rural valley of coastal Mendocino County, Edmeades Vineyards is
donating part of the receipt from the sale of this bottle of Cabernet
Sauvignon to the Anderson Valley Health Center.

Edmeades Vineyards is said to be the "first varietal vineyard" planted in one of the remotest and certainly the rainiest viticultural region in California, the Anderson Valley of coastal Mendocino County.

Established in 1964, Edmeades Vineyards was the project of one physician and horticulturist, Dr. Donald Edmeades, who was determined to prove that fine grapes and flavorful wines could be produced in an area that for too long was thought only suitable for sheep and apples.

Encouraged by the support and counsel of Dr. A.J. Winkler, professor of viticulture at U.C. Davis, Dr. Edmeades proceeded with his plantings of three varieties considered appropriate for the cool Region I: 13 acres of Chardonnay; 15 acres of Gewurztraminer; three acres of French Colombard; and one variety thought adaptable but questionable pending conditions at harvest—five acres of Cabernet Sauvignon. Successive harvest, beginning in 1968, so pleased the doctor (and his clients at Parducci Cellars to whom he sold the wine grapes) that in 1970, he made mental plans to start the winery building. An untimely death in 1972 left the estate to his son and heir, Deron Edmeades.

Inspired by his father's achievements, in 1972 Deron began a two part winery plan which was completed in 1976: conversion of an ancient apple dryer into the "lower winery" and construction of a new redwood facility into the "upper winery." Upon the recommendation of winemaker Jed Steele, the winery was equipped with stainless steel jacketed fermenters, 135 gallon French oak puncheons as well as new crushing, pressing and bottling equipment.

The two sources of wine grapes which have proved most beneficial to Steele's idea of quality come from the 35 acres of estate vines and local Anderson Valley growers. "Approximately 98 percent of our grapes come from the Anderson Valley," says Steele, who points out that Edmeades pioneered the use of Anderson Valley as an appellation of origin, which is used on the label of many of its varietal bottlings.

Edmeades produces Chardonnay, Gewurztraminer, Opal (White Pinot Noir), Zinfandel and Cabernet Sauvignon in its varietal line. The only generic wine made by Edmeades is its Rain Wine, a varying blend based on French Colombard. "We are trying to make a quality product," says Edmeades. "We want to emphasize the Anderson Valley as a distinct climatic region of Mendocino County. It has a cool coastal climate and a long, but unpredictable growing season." For added perspective Steele emphasizes the differences in several grapes from this area such as Chardonnay and Gewurztraminer. "The cool days and the cool nights produce white wines which are higher in acid with extremely clean, delicate varietal tones," says Steele. "The Cabernet Sauvignon, however, appears to be more of a gamble. Some years it may be light, while in other years full and complex but never a heavy wine."

Cresta Blanca Winery

The name Cresta Blanca has had significance for nearly a century in the history of the California wine business. The first Cresta Blanca was founded by San Francisco journalist Charles A. Wetmore in 1872, who became interested in viticulture in the late 1870s while compiling a study on the state's wine industry for the *Alta California*. His investigations revealed that inferior quality grapes were the cause of California's inferior quality wines. Wetmore's continued research took him to the Paris Exposition on behalf of the California State Viticultural Society in 1878. He traveled widely in the vineyards of France, studying winegrowing techniques. A series of articles in the *Alta California* on viticulture aroused the state's agriculturists to action.

This journalist-turned-winegrower had purchased 480 acres of the Rancho El Valle de San Jose for $200 gold coin and named it Cresta Blanca, for the white-crested cliffs above the canyon of the Arroyo del Valle. Armed with a letter from the wife of a pioneer resident, Madame Louis Mel, Wetmore returned to France to visit the Marquis de Lur Saluces, proprietor of Chateau d'Yquem. From him Wetmore obtained cuttings which had made Chateau d'Yquem famous— Semillon, Sauvignon Blanc, Colombard and Muscadelle du Bordelaise. In 1889 Wetmore again returned to France, taking with him some of his first vintages to enter in the Paris Exposition. Out of 17,000 entries, Cresta Blanca took top honors, winning the coveted Grand Prix. The Marquis de Lur Saluces was present at the judging and exclaimed, "The daughter has excelled the mother."

In 1941, Schenley Industries, headed by whiskey scion Lewis Rosensteil, acquired Cresta Blanca from close family associates of the Wetmores. He proceeded to use the prestigious Cresta Blanca name to market their line and popularize other lines owned by Schenley.

North State Street in Ukiah is the site of the present Cresta Blanca Winery in Mendocino County. A new 500,000 case winery has been completed, with fermentation chambers, bottling line, offices and tasting room. The older wood aging cellars were first established as the Mendocino Cooperative. In 1946, it became affiliated with Guild Wineries and Distilleries of Lodi. It wasn't until Guild purchased the Cresta Blanca name from Schenley in 1971 that the Mendocino site was so named. Today grapes are purchased from three areas throughout California: Mendocino County, Santa Barbara and San Luis Obispo.

Cresta Blanca produces a complete line of vintage-dated premium table wines, with either a Santa Barbara or Mendocino appellation of origin for $5.00 a fifth or less. The wines include Pinot Chardonnay, Chenin Blanc, Johannisberg Riesling, French Colombard, Gewurztraminer, Muscato di Canelli, Chablis, Grenache Rose, Blanc de Blanc, Cabernet Sauvignon, Pinot Noir, Zinfandel, Petite Sirah, Gamay Beaujolais, Carnelian and a Mendocino Burgundy. A popular Triple Cream Sherry tops the list of fortified wines made.

Parducci Wine Cellars

MENDOCINO COUNTY
CHARDONNAY

PRODUCED & BOTTLED BY PARDUCCI WINE CELLARS
UKIAH, MENDOCINO COUNTY, CALIFORNIA
ALCOHOL 11.5% BY VOLUME

It is but the oldest wine family in Mendocino County, that of Adolph Parducci, Sr., of Parducci Wine Cellars in Ukiah, that can claim three consecutive generations of winemaking and half a century of experience.

Adolph Parducci, founder, learned winemaking as a boy in Italy from his father, John Parducci, before coming to the United States in 1917. He made Cloverdale in northern Sonoma County the site of his first winery, a small bulk concern supplying individuals, and then altar wines during Prohibition.

By 1931, Parducci established the present winery in a wooded canyon on the 120 acre Pine Mountain Ranch in Mendocino County. Again business was primarily bulk, with some sales by bottle and barrel. In 1961 Adolph resigned and two of his four sons, George and John took over. John shares winemaking with Joe Monostori and is general manager of operations; George handles the financial and administrative responsibilities. Since 1974, the Parducci brothers have been involved in a limited partnership agreement with the Teachers Management and Investment Corporation of Newport Beach, California.

Fine Mendocino County appellation wines, averaging 200,000 cases annually, in the medium price range are made from 250 acres of vines at three ranch sites: Home, Large and Talmage, and from grapes purchased from local growers. The diversity of growing areas has offered Parducci unlimited resources for experimentation.

Parducci Wine Cellars has defined its position in the national marketplace based on several key policies. Mendocino County grapes are promoted as strong on regional character and varietal flavor. This has been impressed upon the consumer and proven in the "taste" of the wines now available. Some examples are the Chardonnay, the semi-dry Chenin Blanc, the best selling French Colombard, the berry-like Zinfandel and the intense Charbono.

"The philosophy of our winemaking is based on the fact that our winemakers are never quite satisfied and are constantly trying to improve our wine, creating new variations and working with new cooperage," says John.

The philosophy of aging has also sparked interest among the winery's followers. All wines are fermented in stainless fermentation units. Whites are traditionally stored in stainless prior to bottling to maintain youth and freshness. Some reds are held in a combination of redwood (an aging barrel that imparts no flavors) for a minimum of three years, and then as in the case of the Petite Sirah and Gamay Beaujolais bottled immediately. The Cabernet Sauvignon, however, along with the Pinot Noir, are aged further in small French oak barrels or larger upright oak tanks.

Cabernet Sauvignons that represent a better year are specified by vineyard such as Talmage or Philo. Rare vintages of exceptional quality are handled separately and called Special Reserve Bottlings.

Fetzer Vineyards

Fetzer
1974
ESTATE BOTTLED • MENDOCINO
CABERNET SAUVIGNON
PRODUCED AND BOTTLED BY
fetzer Vineyards
REDWOOD VALLEY, CALIFORNIA
ALCOHOL 12% BY VOLUME

One hundred twenty-five miles north of San Francisco in Mendocino County lies the over 100-year-old grape growing district known as the Redwood Valley. It was to this valley, located at the headwaters of the Russian River in Ukiah, that former Masonite executive Bernard Fetzer came in 1955 to plant Bordeaux varieties: Cabernet Sauvignon, Sauvignon Blanc and Semillon.

Crops harvested from the 160 acres of vines on the 750 acre ranch were sold to homewinemakers throughout Canada and the United States. So encouraged were clients about their quality homemade wines that in 1968 Fetzer made 2500 cases and founded Fetzer Vineyards.

Modestly priced premium red wines, the Cabernet Sauvignons and Zinfandels being the most highly regarded, established their reputation. In less than 15 years, the success of this once small family operation has mushroomed, twice quadrupling case quantities, to its present 150,000 case size.

As Fetzer enters the ever-growing sophistication of the national wine arena of the 1980's, the entire family has prepared itself to meet, and surpass if they must, their most watchful competitors. The operational structure remains basically family with some new blood. Bernard Fetzer is president and owner. Son John is general manager; daughter Patti is office manager. Mary heads shipping and sales assisted by sisters Teresa and Diane and brother Daniel. Brothers James, Richard and Robert manage production. In 1977, Paul Dolan, a graduate in enology from U.C. Fresno, was hired to upgrade the quality of the premium line for national distribution.

A new 190,000 gallon winery for white wine production has been completed. It has new fermenters, crushers, stemmers, presses, centrifuge, storage area, and 6,000 small American and French oak barrels fill the aging cellar. Forty percent of the production is devoted to white varietals, with emphasis on more readily drinkable wines. They include a barrel-fermented Chardonnay, a Sauvignon Blanc and Pinot Blanc, all of which are oak-aged. The lower alcohol wines, the dry Gewurztraminer, the off-dry Johannisberg Riesing and semi-sweet Muscat Canelli see some or no oak.

Fetzer Vineyards continues to produce its red wines in the original wood and fieldstone winery set into a natural canyon. The styles available offer the consumer a range of tasting experiences from the softer, rounder, more commercial Lake County Cabernet Sauvignon to the Mendocino Gamay Beaujolais and Gamay to the fuller, more pronounced Mendocino Cabernet Sauvignon, Pinot Noir, Zinfandel and Petite Sirah. Vineyard lots are kept separate during processing and throughout aging until blended or bottled individually, pending quality of the wine in cask. Special bottlings include Zinfandels from the Ricetti, Mattern and Lolonis vineyards, and Cabernet Sauvignons from Mendocino and Lake counties.

The impact of Fetzer Vineyards in its new guise is firmly based on use of top quality grapes, stronger winemaking emphasis and tighter control through small barrel aging.

Other Wineries

DACH VINEYARDS

In 1971, Sandra and John Dach left the hills of Los Gatos on the outskirts of San Jose for the rural splendors of the Anderson Valley in Mendocino County.

"We wanted to establish a vineyard, and heard that the Anderson Valley was one of the last Region I growing areas comparable to similar districts in Europe," remarks Sandra Dach, owner.

Husband John had previously been employed at the Jesuit Novitiate Winery in Los Gatos where he had logged experience of all kinds from running the business office to making wine in the cellars. A short-term partnership with several friends, inspired from his love for wine, produced 1000 gallons of wine under the Bear Creek Vineyards label.

Since 1974 Dach Vineyards, located along the California State Highway 128, has been planted to 20 acres of Chardonnay, Gewurztraminer, and Pinot Noir. "We have hope that one year we will establish a small premium estate winery like our neighbors," explains Sandra. For the meantime, a project developing apple orchards has postponed building of the winery, but the eighties promise to hold the beginning of this long-anticipated venture.

McDOWELL VALLEY VINEYARDS

Richard and Karen Keehn of Hopland in Mendocino County are owners with their eight children of what promises to be the only family owned and operated solar winery in America.

The valley to which the Keehns have devoted 10 years of grape growing, located on the 1888 Feliza Fernandez Mexican land grant, dates from the pre-turn-of-the-century as a productive vineyard site. Grapes grew there consistently until Prohibition when they were torn out. After the Dry years, the vines were replanted and sold for bulk production until the sixties. In 1970, the Keehns combined several area ranches to create their 360 acres of estate vines.

Construction commenced on the winery in the spring of 1979, and the first grapes crushed that fall. The 16,000 case winery will feature McDowell Valley appellation premium varietals, many of which are oak-aged. They include: Chardonnay, Riesling, Sauvignon Blanc, Chenin Blanc, French Colombard, Cabernet Sauvignon, Zinfandel, Petite Sirah and Grenache. U.C. Davis master of enology, George Bursick, formerly from Beringer, will work to produce the best wines possible.

Milano

1977
Pacini
Talmage-Mendocino

ZINFANDEL

ALCOHOL 13.9% BY VOLUME
PRODUCED AND BOTTLED BY Milano Winery
HOPLAND, MENDOCINO COUNTY, CALIFORNIA

There is an inexplicable bond that exists when you are high school friends from Ukiah, and your family's family are amongst the early Italian settlers in the Mendocino wine country. Such was the relationship and common heritage shared by James Milone and Gregory Graziano that prompted them to found the Milano Winery in Hopland.

The notion for starting a winery originated in the early seventies while students. "We got this crazy idea that we should be growing grapes and making wine here," says Milone, "and not sending such large quantities out of the county." By 1975, after college, they got the support of their families to restore the hop kiln and make it the winery, as well as to contract out grapes from their vineyards.

Milano Winery will build its reputation on three red varieties: Cabernet Sauvignon, Petite Sirah and Zinfandel, all from 100 percent varietals. Small quantities are available of Gamay Beaujolais, Chardonnay, Sauvignon Blanc and Chenin Blanc. The vineyard-designate Zinfandels are by far the best wines made.

Appendix

ALEXANDER VALLEY VINEYARDS - Page 105
    Address: 8644 Highway 128, Healdsburg 95448
    Phone: (707) 433-7209
    Hours: 10-5 daily
    Facilities: tasting, sales, tours by appointment
    Winemaker: Harry (Hank) Wetzel, III
    Vineyards: 240 acres
    Volume: 10,000 cases annually

BANDIERA WINES - Page 137
    Address: 155 Cherry Creek Rd., Cloverdale 95476
    Phone: (707) 894-2352
    Hours: by appointment
    Facilities: sales
    Winemaker: Chris Bilbro
    Vineyards: none
    Volume: 8,000 cases annually

BUENA VISTA WINERY & VINEYARDS - Page 41
    Address: 18000 Old Winery Rd., Sonoma 95476
    Phone: (707) 938-1266
    Hours: 10-5 daily
    Facilities: tasting, sales, self-guided tour
    Winemaker: Richard Williams
    Vineyards: 700 acres
    Volume: 55,000 cases annually

DAVIS BYNUM WINERY - Page 75
    Address: 8075 Westside Rd., Healdsburg 95448
    Phone: (707) 433-5852
    Hours: by appointment
    Facilities: sales only, tours by appt.
    Winemaker: Davis Bynum
    Vineyards: none
    Volume: 15,000 cases annually

CAMBIASO WINERY & VINEYARDS - Page 89
    Address: 1141 Grant Ave., Healdsburg 95448
    Phone: (707) 433-5508
    Hours: 10-4 daily except holidays
    Facilities: sales, tasting by appt.
    Winemaker: Robert Fredson
    Vineyards: 35 acres
    Volume: 80,000 cases annually

CHATEAU ST. JEAN - Page 55
    Address: 8555 Sonoma Highway, Kenwood 95452
    Phone: (707) 833-4134
    Hours: 10-4:30 daily
    Facilities: tasting, sales, tours by appt.
    Winemaker: Richard Arrowood
    Vineyards: 124 acres
    Volume: 40,000-50,000 cases annually

CLOS DU BOIS - Page 139
Address: 764 W. Dry Creek Rd., Healdsburg
Phone: (415) 456-7310
Hours: by appointment only
Facilities: none available to the public
Winemaker: Tom Hobart
Vineyards: 300 acres
Volume: 10,000-20,000 cases annually

CRESTA BLANCA WINERY - Page 149
Address: 2399 N. State St., Ukiah 95482
Phone: (707) 462-0565
Hours: 9-5 daily
Facilities: sales, tours by request
Winemaker: Gerald Furman
Vineyards: cooperative
Volume: 500,000 cases annually

DACH VINEYARDS - Page 155
Address: P.O. Box 86, Philo 95466
Phone: (707) 895-3245
Hours: not open to the public
Facilities: none
Winemaker: John Dach
Vineyards: 20 acres
Volume: not disclosed

DEHLINGER WINERY - Page 63
Address: 6300 Guerneville Rd., Sebastopol 95472
Phone: (707) 823-2378
Hours: by appointment only
Facilities: none available to the public
Winemaker: Tom Dehlinger
Vineyards: 14 acres
Volume: 5,000 cases annually

DRY CREEK VINEYARD, INC. - Page 95
Address: 3770 Lambert Bridge Rd., Healdsburg 95448
Phone: (707) 433-1000
Hours: 10:30-4:30 daily
Facilities: tours, tasting, sales
Winemaker: David S. Stare
Vineyards: 50 acres
Volume: 22,000 cases annually

EDMEADES VINEYARDS - Page 147
Address: 5500 Ca. Ste. Hwy. 128, Philo 95466
Phone: (707) 895-3232
Hours: 10-6 daily summer; 11-5 daily winter
Facilities: tasting, tours, sales
Winemaker: Jed Steele
Vineyards: 35 acres
Volume: 8,000-10,000 cases annually

FETZER VINEYARDS - Page 153
Address: 1150 Bel Arbes Rd., Redwood Valley 95470
Phone: (707) 485-8998
Hours: by appt. 485-8802; Hopland tasting 9:30-5 daily
Facilities: tours by appt, tasting daily at Hopland
Winemaker: Paul Dolan
Vineyards: 160 acres
Volume: 100,000 cases annually

FIELD STONE WINERY - Page 103
Address: 10075 Ste. Hwy. 128, Healdsburg 95448
Phone: (707) 433-7266
Hours: 9-5 daily
Facilities: tasting, tours, sales, picnic area
Winemaker: William Arbois
Vineyards: 140 acres
Volume: 10,000 cases annually

FOPPIANO VINEYARDS - Page 85
  Address: 12707 Old Redwood Hwy., Healdsburg
  Phone: (707) 433-1937
  Hours: 10-4:30 daily
  Facilities: tours by appt., tasting, sales
  Winemaker: Rod Foppiano
  Vineyards: 200 acres
  Volume: 200,000 cases annually

GEYSER PEAK WINERY - Page 121
  Address: Canyon Rd. exit from 101, Geyserville
  Phone: (707) 433-6585
  Hours: 10-5 daily
  Facilities: tours by appt., sales, tasting
  Winemaker: Armand Bussone
  Vineyards: 625 acres
  Volume: 450,000 cases annually

GRAND CRU VINEYARDS - Page 53
  Address: 1 Vintage Lane, Glen Ellen 95442
  Phone: (707) 996-8100
  Hours: 10-5 weekends only
  Facilities: tasting, tours, sales
  Winemaker: Robert L. Magnani
  Vineyards: 30 acres
  Volume: 20,000 cases annually

GRAND PACIFIC VINEYARD COMPANY - Page 32
  Address: 134 Paul Dr. #9, San Rafael 94901
  Phone: (415) 457-4791
  Hours: by appointment
  Facilities: tasting, tours, sales
  Winemaker: Richard Dye
  Vineyards: none
  Volume: 3,000 cases annually

GUNDLACH BUNDSCHU WINE CO. - Page 37
  Address: 3773 Thornsberry Rd., Vineburg 95487
  Phone: (707) 938-5277
  Hours: 12-4:30 Friday, Saturday & Sunday
  Facilities: tours, tasting, sales
  Winemaker: John Merritt, Jr.
  Vineyards: 300 acres
  Volume: 10,000 cases annually

HACIENDA WINE CELLARS - Page 39
  Address: 1000 Vineyard Ln, Box 416, Sonoma 95476
  Phone: (707) 938-3220
  Hours: 10-5 daily
  Facilities: tours by appt., tasting, sales
  Winemaker: Steve MacRostie
  Vineyards: 130 acres
  Volume: 20,000 cases annually

HANZELL VINEYARDS - Page 49
  Address: 18596 Lomita Ave., Sonoma 95476
  Phone: (707) 996-3860
  Hours: not open to the public
  Facilities: tours by appt., sales, no tasting
  Winemaker: Robert Sessions
  Vineyards: 32 acres
  Volume: 2,000 cases annually

J.J. HARASZTHY & SON - Page 58
  Address: P.O. Box 375, Sonoma 95476
  Phone: (707) 996-3040
  Hours: 9-4 daily
  Facilities: tours possible
  Wine Blender: Val Haraszthy
  Vineyards: none
  Volume: 3,000 cases annually

HOP KILN WINERY - Page 77
  Address: 6050 Westside Rd., Healdsburg 95448
  Phone: (707) 433-6491
  Hours: weekends 10-5 daily; weekdays by appt.
  Facilities: tours, tasting, sales
  Winemaker: Dr. L. Martin Griffin, Jr.
  Vineyards: 65 acres
  Volume: 4,500 cases annually

HUSCH VINEYARDS - Page 145
  Address: 4900 Ca. Ste. Hwy 128, Philo 95466
  Phone: (707) 895-3216
  Hours: 10-5 daily
  Facilities: tours, tasting, sales
  Winemaker: Tony Husch
  Vineyards: 25 acres
  Volume: 6,500 cases annually

IRON HORSE RANCH & VINEYARD - Page 90
  Address: 9786 Ross Station Rd., Sebastopol
  Phone: (707) 887-1909
  Hours: by appointment only
  Facilities: by appointment only
  Winemaker: Forest Tancer
  Vineyards: 150 acres
  Volume: 6,000 cases annually

ITALIAN SWISS COLONY - Page 129
  Address: Asti 95425
  Phone: (707) 894-2541
  Hours: 10-5 daily
  Facilities: tours, tasting, sales
  Winemaker: Thomas Eddy
  Vineyards: 600 acres

JADE MOUNTAIN WINERY - Page 133
  Address: 1335 Hiatt Rd., Cloverdale 95425
  Phone: please write
  Hours: not open to the public
  Facilities: none
  Winemaker: Dr. Douglass Cartwright
  Vineyards: 35 acres
  Volume: 2,000 cases annually

JOHNSON'S ALEXANDER VALLEY WINES - Page 107
  Address: 8333 Ca. Ste. Hwy 128, Healdsburg 95448
  Phone: (707) 433-2319
  Hours: 10-5 daily; monthly Sunday open house
  Facilities: tours, tasting, sales
  Winemaker: Tom Johnson
  Vineyards: 70 acres
  Volume: 10,000 cases annually

JORDAN VINEYARDS - Page 138
  Address: P.O. Box 878, Healdsburg 95448
  Phone: (707) 433-6955
  Hours: no hours
  Facilities: none available to the public
  Winemaster: Michael Rowan
  Vineyards: 250 acres
  Volume: 12,000 cases annually

KENWOOD VINEYARDS - Page 57
  Address: 9592 Sonoma Highway, Kenwood 95452
  Phone: (707) 833-5891
  Hours: 9-5 daily
  Facilities: tasting, sales, tours by appt. only
  Winemakers: Dr. Robert Kozlowski & Michael Lee
  Vineyards: 20 acres owned; 100 under contract
  Volume: 30,000 cases annually

KISTLER VINEYARDS - Page 58
Address: 2995 Nelligan Rd., Glen Ellen
Phone: (707) 833-4462
Hours: not open to the public
Facilities: none available
Winemaker: Stephen Kistler
Vineyards: 40 acres
Volume: 4,000-6,000 cases annually

F. KORBEL & BROS. - Page 71
Address: Guerneville 95446
Phone: (707) 887-2294
Hours: 9:45-5:30 daily
Facilities: tours, tasting, sales
Champagne-master: Adolf Heck
Vineyards: 600 acres
Volume: 250,000 cases champagne; 10,000 wine

LANDMARK VINEYARDS - Page 81
Address: 9150 Los Amigos Rd., Windsor 95492
Phone: (707) 838-9466
Hours: 1-5 Wed. & Fri.; 10-5 Sat. & Sun.
Facilities: tours and sales
Winemaker: William R. Mabry, III
Vineyards: 87 acres
Volume: 10,000-15,000 cases annually

LAMBERT BRIDGE - Page 97
Address: 4085 W. Dry Creek Rd., Healdsburg
Phone: (707) 433-5855
Hours: by appointment only
Facilities: sales by case only, tours by appt.
Winemaker: Nick Martin
Vineyards: 80 acres
Volume: 10,000 cases annually

LYTTON SPRINGS WINERY - Page 139
Address: 650 Lytton Springs, Rd., Healdsburg
Phone: (707) 433-7721
Hours: 9-5 daily
Facilities: tasting
Winemaker: Bura Walters
Vineyards: 49.22 acres
Volume: 3,000-5,000 cases annually

MARK WEST VINEYARDS - Page 69
Address: 7000 Trenton-Healdsburg Rd., Forestville
Phone: (707) 544-5813
Hours: weekdays 8-5 daily; weekends by appt.
Facilities: tours & sales only
Winemaker: Joan Ellis
Vineyards: 62 acres
Volume: 5,500 cases annually

MARTINI & PRATI - Page 65
Address: 2191 Laguna Rd., Santa Rosa 95401
Phone: (707) 823-2404
Hours: 9-4 daily Monday-Friday
Facilities: tasting, sales, no tours
Winemaker: Frank Vanucci
Vineyards: 70 acres
Volume: 500,000 gallons annually

MATANZAS CREEK WINERY - Page 90
Address: 6097 Bennett Valley Rd., Santa Rosa
Phone: (707) 542-8242
Hours: write for appt.
Facilities: sales through mailing list
Winemaker: Merry Edwards
Vineyards: 50 acres
Volume: 3,500 cases annually

MAZZONI WINERY - Page 125
    Address: 23645 Redwood Highway, Cloverdale
    Phone: (707) 857-3691
    Hours: 9-5 daily
    Facilities: case sales only
    Winemaker: Fred Mazzoni
    Vineyards: none
    Volume: 2,000 cases annually

MCDOWELL VALLEY VINEYARDS - Page 155
    Address: 3811 Hwy. 175, Hopland 95449
    Phone: (707) 744-1774
    Hours: by appointment
    Facilities: open in 1981, tours by appt.
    Winemaker: George Bursick
    Vineyards: 360 acres
    Volume: 16,000 to 25,000 cases in several years

MILANO WINERY - Page 156
    Address: 14594 S. Hwy. 101, Hopland 95449
    Phone: (707) 744-1396
    Hours: 9-4 daily
    Facilities: tasting, sales & tours
    Winemakers: Gregory Graziano & Jim Milone
    Vineyards: none
    Volume: 5,000 cases annually

MILL CREEK VINEYARDS - Page 79
    Address: 1401 Westside Rd., Healdsburg 95448
    Phone: (707) 433-5098
    Hours: 10-4 weekdays
    Facilities: sales, tours by appt., no tasting
    Winemaker: James Kreck
    Vineyards: 65 acres
    Volume: 10,000 cases annually

NAVARRO VINEYARDS - Page 143
    Address: 5601 Ca. Ste. Hwy 128, Philo 94708
    Phone: (707) 895-3686
    Hours: 10-5 daily Mon.-Fri. only
    Facilities: tours by appt. only, tasting, sales
    Winemaker: Edward (Ted) Bennett
    Vineyards: 55 acres
    Volume: 7,000 cases annually

NERVO WINERY - Page 117
    Address: Independence exit off 101, Geyserville 95441
    Phone: (707) 857-3417
    Hours: 10-5 daily
    Facilities: tasting, sales, picnic area
    Winemaker: Armand Bussone
    Vineyards: 137 acres
    Volume: sales outlet only

NOB HILL CELLARS - Page 33
    Address: 200 Gate 5 Rd., Sausalito
    Phone: (415) 771-5065
    Hours: by appointment only
    Facilities: tasting, sales in case lots
    Winemaker: Gil Nickel
    Vineyards: none
    Volume: 5,000 cases annually

PARDUCCI WINE CELLARS - Page 151
    Address: 501 Parducci Road, Ukiah 95482
    Phone: (707) 462-3828
    Hours: 9-5 daily
    Facilities: tours, tasting, sales
    Winemakers: John Parducci & Joseph Monostori
    Vineyards: 300 acres
    Volume: 200,000 cases annually

PASTORI WINERY - Page 123
    Address: 23189 Redwood Hwy., Cloverdale 95425
    Phone: (707) 857-3418
    Hours: 9-5 daily
    Facilities: tasting, sales, tours
    Winemaker: Frank Pastori
    Vineyards: 50 acres
    Volume: 5,000 cases annually

J. PEDRONCELLI WINERY - Page 119
    Address: 1220 Canyon Rd., Geyserville 95441
    Phone: (707) 857-3619
    Hours: 10-5 daily
    Facilities: tasting, sales, no tours
    Winemaker: John Pedroncelli
    Vineyards: 135 acres
    Volume: 100,000 cases annually

PRESTON VINEYARDS - Page 101
    Address: 9282 W. Dry Creek Rd., Healdsburg
    Phone: (707) 433-4748
    Hours: by appointment only
    Facilities: tasting & sales by appt. only
    Winemaker: Louis D. Preston
    Vineyards: 70 acres
    Volume: 3,500 cases annually

A. RAFANELLI WINERY - Page 99
    Address: 4685 W. Dry Creek Rd., Healdsburg
    Phone: (707) 433-1385
    Hours: by appointment only
    Facilities: sales, no tours or tasting
    Winemaker: Americo Rafanelli
    Vineyards: 25 acres
    Volume: 3,000 cases annually

REGE WINE CO. - Page 135
    Address: 26700 Dutcher Creek Rd., Cloverdale
    Phone: (707) 894-2953
    Hours: 9-5 daily
    Facilities: tasting & sales
    Winemaker: Eugene Rene
    Vineyards: 84 acres
    Volume: 30,000 cases annually

RIVER OAKS VINEYARDS - Page 91
    Address: 36 Mill St., Healdsburg 95448
    Phone: (707) 433-5663
    Hours: by appointment only
    Facilities: none
    Winemaker: Frank Woods
    Vineyards: 1700 acres
    Volume: not disclosed

SAUSAL WINERY - Page 109
    Address: 7370 Ca. Ste. Hwy. 128, Healdsburg
    Phone: (707) 433-2285
    Hours: not open to the public
    Facilities: none available
    Winemaker: David Demostene
    Vineyards: 150 acres
    Volume: 50,000 cases annually

SEBASTIANI VINEYARDS - Page 45
    Address: 389 Fourth St. E., Sonoma 95476
    Phone: (707) 938-5532
    Hours: 10-5 daily
    Facilities: tours, tasting, sales
    Winemaker: August Sebastiani
    Vineyards: 400 acres
    Volume: 3,000,000 cases annually

SIMI WINERY - Page 111
    Address: 16275 Healdsburg Ave., Healdsburg
    Phone: (707) 433-6981
    Hours: 10-5 daily
    Facilities: tours, tasting, sales
    Winemaker: none presently
    Vineyards: none
    Volume: 135,000 cases annually by 1985

SONOMA VINEYARDS - Page 83
    Address: 11455 Old Redwood Hwy., Windsor
    Phone: (707) 433-6511
    Hours: 10-5 daily
    Facilities: tours by appt., tasting, sales
    Winemaker: Rodney D. Strong
    Vineyards: 650 acres
    Volume: 250,000 cases annually

SOTOYOME WINERY - Page 87
    Address: 641 Limmerick Lane, Healdsburg 95448
    Phone: (707) 433-2001
    Hours: by appointment only
    Facilities: tours, tasting, sales
    Winemaker: John C. Stampfl
    Vineyards: 15 acres
    Volume: 4,000 cases annually

SOUVERAIN CELLARS - Page 113
    Address: 400 Souverain Rd., Geyserville 95411
    Phone: (707) 433-6918
    Hours: 10-5 daily
    Facilities: tours, tasting, sales
    Winemaker: William Bonetti
    Vineyards: 3 acres
    Volume: 500,000 cases annually

ROBERT STEMMLER WINERY - Page 139
    Address: 3805 Lambert Bridge Rd., Healdsburg
    Phone: (707) 433-6334
    Hours: by appointment only
    Facilities: sales, no tours or tasting
    Winemaker: Robert Stemmler
    Vineyards: 3 acres
    Volume: 2,000 cases annually

JOSEPH SWAN VINEYARDS - Page 67
    Address: 2916 Laguna Rd., Forestville 95436
    Phone: (707) 546-7711
    Hours: not open to the public
    Facilities: none available
    Winemaker: Joseph Swan
    Vineyards: 10 acres
    Volume: 2,000 cases annually

TRENTADUE VINEYARDS - Page 115
    Address: 19170 Redwood Hwy., Geyserville 95441
    Phone: (707) 433-3104
    Hours: 10-5 daily
    Facilities: tasting, sales, gift shop
    Winemakers: Leo & Victor Trentadue
    Vineyards: 200 acres
    Volume: 15,000 cases annually

VALLEY OF THE MOON WINERY - Page 51
    Address: 777 Madrone Rd., Glen Ellen 95442
    Phone: (707) 996-6941
    Hours: 10-5 daily except Thursday
    Facilities: tasting, sales, no tours
    Winemakers: Harry Parducci & Otto Toschi
    Vineyards: 200 acres
    Volume: 90,000 cases annually

VIEWS LAND COMPANY - Page 59
    Address: 18701 Gehricke Rd., Sonoma 94576
    Phone: (707) 938-3768
    Hours: not open to the public
    Facilities: none available
    Winemaker: Walter Benson
    Vineyards: 15 acres
    Volume: 3,500 cases annually

VINA VISTA VINEYARDS - Page 127
    Address: Chianti Rd., Geyserville, CA 95441
    Phone: (707) 857-3722 or (415) 969-3160
    Hours: by appointment weekends only
    Facilities: tours, tasting, sales
    Winemaker: Keith D. Nelson
    Vineyards: none
    Volume: 5,000 cases annually

WILLOWSIDE VINEYARDS - Page 91
    Address: 1670 Willowside Rd., Santa Rosa
    Phone: (707) 544-7504
    Hours: by appointment only
    Facilities: sales
    Winemaker: Berle Beliz
    Vineyards: 24 acres
    Volume: 7,000 cases annually

WOODBURY WINERY - Page 32
    Address: 32 Woodland Ave., San Rafael 94901
    Phone: (415) 454-2355
    Hours: by appointment only
    Facilities: sales, tours, & tasting
    Winemaker: Russell Woodbury
    Vineyards: none
    Volume: 1,000 cases annually

ZD WINERY - Page 59
    Address: 20735 Burndale Rd., Sonoma 95476
    Phone: (707) 539-9137
    Hours: by appointment only
    Facilities: sales, tours, tasting by appt.
    Winemakers: Gino Zepponi & Norman de Leuze
    Vineyards: none
    Volume: 5,000 cases annually

The definitive annual editions of California Wine Country - Napa Valley (Vol. I), Sonoma & Mendocino (Vol. II), and Central Coast (Vol. III) are now available! Absolutely up to date and all inclusive, the Wine Book Series explores every existing winery in the coastal wine growing regions from Mendocino to Santa Barbara. Each handsome 7¼ x 9 inch volume is extensively illustrated with lithographs by famed California artist Sebastian Titus. Special emphasis has been given to the colorful and sometimes enigmatic winemakers and their wines. Each edition contains detailed area maps pinpointing exact winery locations and a complete appendix providing easy reference to vital information. $6.95 per volume

WINE TOUR GUIDE SERIES

For those fortunate enough to visit California's wine growing regions, we offer the "Wine Tour" Series. These three books covering the regions Napa Valley, Sonoma & Mendocino, & the Central Coast are companions to our "Wine Book" Series. These are complete guidebooks for the wine traveler with a chapter on FOOD which reviews noteworthy restaurants and

for picnickers, a listing of local shops purveying provisions. A chapter on LODGING reviews the best inns, resorts & campgrounds. Included are many detailed road maps and points of interest. The WINERY chapter lists all the relevant information such as address, phone number, hours, facilities and includes specific directions on how to get there. These are the only books of their kind and are a must for the wine country traveler. $2.95 each